Warships and Navies 1973

Frontispiece: **A 'Harrier' hovering and about to land on the Ark Royal**   *[MoD, RN, Official*

Warships and Navies
1973

Edited by
Anthony J. Watts

LONDON
IAN ALLAN

First Published 1972

SBN: 7110 0385 8

© Ian Allan 1972

Published by Ian Allan Ltd, Shepperton, Surrey
and printed in the United Kingdom by
A. Wheaton & Co, Exeter

Contents

Introduction 7

The Major Powers *by Raymond V. B. Blackman, MBE, C.Eng, MI.Mar.E, FRINA* 9

The Royal Navy in the Seventies *by Desmond Wettern* 27

A Maritime VTOL Aircraft? *by Anthony J. Watts* 38

Ship-Borne Air Support—the Hybrid Cruiser/Carrier *by Captain Donald Macintyre, DSO* 40

The Tiger Class *by P. A. Vicary* 51

Ship Missiles—the surface-to-surface problem *by John Marriott* 55

The County Class Destroyer *by Anthony J. Watts* 68

A Life on the Ocean Wave *by Anthony J. Watts* 73

New Destroyers of the Royal Navy *by Anthony J. Watts* 77

The Dartmouth Cadet *by Sub-Lieutenants R. Clare and A. Piška* 79

Life in a Polaris Submarine *by Lieutenant-Commander A. J. R. Watson, RN* 89

Replenishment at Sea *by Anthony J. Watts* 97

The Royal Navy at Sea *by Anthony J. Watts* 109

Vosper Thornycroft Frigates *by Anthony J. Watts* 113

Ship-Borne Helicopters *by J. D. Brown* 117

H.M.S. Rapid *by P. A. Vicary* 128

1972 Defence Estimates and the Royal Navy—A Critical Survey *by Anthony J. Watts* 130

Introduction

Over the last decade the warships and navies of the world have undergone dramatic changes. The warships of today carry vast radar arrays, numerous missile launchers in places where formerly guns were mounted, and in some cases even lack funnels. With so many visual changes having taken place in the silhouettes of warships, it is not surprising to find that revolutions have also taken place within the hulls of these new warships. Not least among the changes are those pertaining to propulsion units. The gas turbine is slowly superseding the ordinary steam turbine, not only for high speed propulsion, but also for cruising purposes. In some vessels, especially in submarines where it has revolutionised underwater warfare and brought about the emergence of the 'true' submarine, the nuclear reactor has gradually gained importance as a new method of propulsion. Other changes include new messing arrangements, the cafeteria system proving popular, and the replacement of the hammock by bunk beds. Computers have also become a vital piece of equipment for modern warships, the human brain being incapable of rapidly solving the numerous arithmetical problems associated with the firing of guided missiles.

Not only have the ships and living conditions on board changed vastly over the last ten years, but so also have the whole organisation of naval forces. The capital ship today is no longer the battleship, or even the aircraft carrier, but the nuclear powered hunter-killer submarine. Today's frigates and destroyers have offensive and defensive capabilities far in excess of anything ever dreamed of during World War II, and in firepower exceed even cruisers in destructive power. Of the major powers, only the United States now retains a large carrier fleet.

With the coming of the H-bomb a new dimension entered warfare. The old theories of the balance of power have been completely altered, and a terrible weapon of destruction hangs like the sword of Damocles over the whole world. The major powers have come to the conclusion that the only way to prevent a nuclear holocaust is to match nuclear weapon for nuclear weapon, with any possible foe. At first this was accomplished by either landbased Intercontinental Ballistic Missiles or airborne H-bombs, but latterly this task has been taken over by the nuclear powered submarine. This was the 'ultimate deterrent', or so it was thought until the last year or so, since when some doubt has been cast on the total surprise potential of the Polaris type nuclear powered submarine. As a result of the heat generated by these large submarines, and the greater sensitivity of infra-red detection devices mounted in spy satellites, it may now be possible to track nuclear powered submarines from the fringes of space.

The aim of this first edition of Warships and Navies is to reflect in articles and pictures this ever-changing pattern that is evolving in the various navies of the world. It is hoped that this new venture will become a regular yearly contribution to the field of naval writing, and will appeal not only to the professional seaman, but also the layman, and in fact to anyone with an interest in naval matters. With such a book as this, dealing with the most modern developments and future plans of navies there is always the possibility that material may become outdated. All the facts quoted within the articles were, as far as is known, correct at the time of going to press.

A.J.W.

The opinions expressed in the articles are those of the writers and not necessarily those of any official body.

HMS *Bulwark*–Britain's first commando carrier.

The Major Powers

RAYMOND V. B. BLACKMAN, MBE,
C.ENG, MI MAR E., FRINA

Editor of *Janes' Fighting Ships*

In former days it was probably true to say that a major power was a country which possessed so many warships of such powerful types that its navy constituted a deterrent against any other country going to war. This was the old conception of a deterrent, the peace-time or cold-war deterrent, although the actual word 'deterrent' was not then used.

Today the word 'deterrent' has a meaning of different degree. It means a nuclear deterrent, that is submarines (or indeed surface ships or aircraft or any other suitable military vehicle) of such devastating power, not only nuclear powered, but armed with nuclear warheads, that they constitute a deterrent against any country going to war. Which is returning to the original premise or first principles; that countries which can build and maintain vessels or machines capable of wielding nuclear missiles to constitute a viable deterrent are major powers.

But assuming that nuclear weapons will never be used again, and they will have failed in their purpose if ever they are, the larger maritime countries still need a peace-time deterrent which is capable of preventing, or stopping, brush-fire wars before they get out of hand and possibly lead to all-out war, which might tempt some megolomaniac to poop off a nuclear missile.

For a hundred years, until World War II, Great Britain possessed the largest and most powerful navy the world had ever seen, and because it constituted a deterrent and gave the United Kingdom and the British Empire the strongest voice in the counsels of the world, it kept the *Pax Britannica*.

Between the two great wars Great Britain and the United States of America nudged each other towards parity, but at the beginning of World War II Great Britain still had the largest navy.

But although some fifteen months after the outbreak of World War II the might of the United States' Navy was destroyed by the Japanese Fleet Air Arm at Pearl Harbor, the United States, which was thereby precipitated into the war, put such a spurt into emergency warship construction thenceforth, that by the end of World War II it had outpaced the Royal Navy of Great Britain, and finished hostilities with the largest navy in the world.

After World War II there was a massive rundown of the British Navy, most of the pre-war ships and a large proportion of the war-built tonnage have been scrapped, sold, or transferred to other navies, while the Unites States continued to run a large majority of its war-built ships and many are still in service to this very day.

At the same time the Soviet Union, which finished World War II with few serviceable warships, started to build up a new navy with professional dedication and progressive acceleration, especially in the submarine field initially, and then in the sphere of rocketry, until the Soviet Navy overtook the British Navy, and Russia became the second naval power, Great Britain dropping to third place.

Thus the navies of the three big victorious nations have dramatically changed their positions and the balance of power. The size and positions of the defeated navies have also drastically altered. France came back into naval pre-eminence largely by her own pride and efforts, and Germany, Italy and Japan, all of whom had been forced to surrender their warships to the Allied Powers for division among the latter at the end of World War II, were subsequently rejuvenated navy-wise, largely under the aegis of the United States, and today all three have very creditable up-and-coming fleets.

Sadly, however, it looks as if the Royal Navy is to suffer yet another setback, and will, owing to imbalance of priorities and political expediency, have to drop to fourth place

9

among the 100 navies of the world. For while British fixed-wing aircraft carriers are being phased out, leaving only one in commission, French aircraft carriers are continuing to remain in service; and while Great Britain has four deterrent submarines France aims to have five.

But for proper comparison of the state of the navies of the four major powers having a nuclear deterrent we must examine their hardware and balance in more detail:

It is probably not universally appreciated that at the present time there are no fewer than 200 nuclear powered submarines afloat in the navies of the, United States of America, the Soviet Union, Great Britain and France.

Approximately half of this total number of nuclear powered true submarines were designed as, and intended for, the role of strategic warfare ships, and the remainder were specifically constructed as fleet (or standard, or 'straight', or 'attack') submarines —according to the country, and as deep-sea hunter-killers for anti-submarine warfare.

In the comparatively short period of only seventeen years the nuclear powered true submarine (true submarine as opposed to a submersible torpedo boat) has progressed with remarkable speed and acceleration from an embryonic scientific concept to a realistic strategic deterrent, and almost entirely under the aegis of United States naval and military technology.

When the USS Nautilus signalled the momentous message: 'Underway on nuclear power' history was made. The date was January 17th, 1955. This vessel was the fore-runner of an underwater fleet which today decides the precedence of navies and the balance of power of nations.

The nuclear powered submarine Nautilus was not only the first true submarine in the world, she was also the world's first nuclear powered ship, and the first nuclear powered vehicle of any kind.

Built by the Electric Boat division of the General Dynamics Corporation, Groton, Connecticut, the Nautilus had a submerged displacement of 4,040 tons with a length of 327.7ft and a beam of 27.6ft. Her power plant consisted of one pressurised water-cooled nuclear reactor and two Westinghouse steam turbines of approximately 15,000 shaft horse power turning two shafts and developing a speed of some twenty knots on the surface and well over twenty knots submerged. She was armed with six 21in. torpedo tubes forward and carried torpedoes for anti-submarine warfare. Her full complement was 105, comprising ten officers and 95 enlisted men.

Thereafter the progress of nuclear powered submarine construction in the United States Navy evolved and developed quite rapidly through a succession of differing types in single or series production, towards standard-isation and perfection in the 'attack' or anti-submarine role.

The first nuclear powered submarine was followed by a second and dissimilar prototype, the USS Seawolf, in 1957, the four nuclear powered attack submarines of the 'Skate' class in 1957 to 1959, the nuclear powered radar-picket submarine Triton (now attack) in 1959, which was, and still is, the longest submarine ever built, with an overall length of 447.5ft, and a submerged displacement of 7,780 tons, powered by two nuclear reactors and two steam turbines aggregating approxi-mately 34,000 shaft horse power and equal to a speed of 27 knots on the surface and twenty knots submerged, and the nuclear powered guided missile submarine Halibut (now research) in 1960.

The six nuclear powered attack submarines of the 'Skipjack' class appeared between 1959 and 1961 (Scorpion of this class was lost in 1968), the nuclear powered attack submarine Tullibee, specifically designed for anti-sub-marine operations, in 1960, the fourteen nuclear powered attack submarines of the 'Permit' class from 1961–1968 (Thresher of this class was lost in 1963), the nuclear powered attack submarine Narwhal (the largest 'straight' or standard SSN yet con-structed by the United States Navy, slightly shorter than the pioneers Nautilus and Seawolf, but broader, deeper and heavier with a sub-

Will Rogers, the last to be completed of the 31 nuclear powered ballistic missile submarines of the 'Lafayette' class. With a displacement of 8,250 tons (surface) these are the largest underwater craft so far built.

merged displacement of 5,350 tons) in 1969, and 33 nuclear powered attack submarines of the 'Sturgeon' class between 1966 and 1972.

In the meantime, however, the evolution and development of nuclear powered *and* ballistic missile armed submarines had been proceeding along practically similar lines in a remarkably energetic manner, and to save designing and drawing board time a short cut was contrived, which resulted in initially two, and successively a whole class of five nuclear powered ballistic missile armed submarines, three more having been constructed quickly, all five in fact having been completed in an average of approximately two years only.

The USS *George Washington* was the first

nuclear powered submarine and the first ship in the western world to be armed with fleet ballistic missiles. The United States Navy had already ordered that the nuclear powered 'attack' or 'straight' submarine which had just been started as SSN 589 was to be completed as a missile submarine, and accordingly this hull was redesignated SSBN 598 and continued construction as the *George Washington* which, like *Nautilus*, made history as a revolutionary prototype.

The twin of the *George Washington*, subsequently named the *Patrick Henry*, was similarly re-ordered at the end of 1957, all the materials in her construction having been intended originally for the not yet begun

Russian 'N' class nuclear powered submarine
hunter-killer. Armed with six 21-inch torpedo tubes
in the bow and four 16-inch aft.

nuclear powered attack submarine SSN 590, and she was then built as the SSBN 599. Both the prototype nuclear powered fleet ballistic missile armed submarine *George Washington* and her first sister ship *Patrick Henry*, were built by General Dynamics (Electric Boat Division).

These two submarines, laid down on November 1st, 1957 (*George Washington*), and May 27th, 1958 (*Patrick Henry*), and commissioned on December 30th, 1959, and April 9th, 1960, respectively (an average period of construction of exactly two years only, a remarkable achievement) and the three sister ships to complete this first class of SSBNs were all built to a modified 'Skipjack' design, but with an extension of nearly 130ft having been fitted in to the originally planned length in order to accommodate sixteen fleet ballistic missiles in two parallel rows of eight vertical tubes abreast sited amidships, as well as fire

control gear and navigational equipment, plus auxiliary machinery.

The third ship of this historic class, the *Theodore Roosevelt*, SSBN 600, was laid down at the Mare Island Naval Shipyard on May 20th, 1958, and commissioned on February 13th, 1961. The fourth vessel was constructed by the Newport News Shipbuilding & DD Company, having been begun on August 25th, 1958, and commissioned on September 16th, 1960, as the *Robert E. Lee*, SSBN 601. The fifth unit was the USS *Abraham Lincoln*, SSBN 602, laid down at the Portsmouth Naval Shipyard on Novemeber 1st, 1958, and commissioned on March 11th, 1961.

All five nuclear powered fleet ballistic missile armed submarines of the 'George Washington' class have a submerged displacement of 6,700 tons submerged with an overall length of 381.7ft, a beam of 33ft and a draught of 29ft. Their power plant comprises one

Nuclear powered ballistic missile submarine
'*Revenge*' 7,500 tons (surface), the last of the four
British Polaris submarines.　　　*[MoD, RN, Official*

French nuclear powered ballistic missile submarine *Le Redoutable,* the first French nuclear powered submarine. Carries 16 Polaris type missiles with a range of 1,900 miles, *[French Navy, Official*

pressurised water-cooled nuclear reactor (S5W type by Westinghouse) and one geared steam turbine by General Electric turning one shaft and developing a speed of twenty knots on the surface and approximately thirty knots submerged.

These first five SSBNs were originally armed with the POLARIS A-1 ballistic missiles with a range of 1,380 statute miles, but all have now been refitted to fire the improved POLARIS A-3 missiles with a range of 2,880 statute miles. They are also fitted with six 21in torpedo tubes forward. Their complement is 112, comprising 12 officers and 100 enlisted men. Each submarine has two separate crews, designated the 'Blue' crew and the 'Gold' crew, who alternate on successive two-month patrols.

The succeeding five nuclear powered fleet ballistic missile armed submarines, known as the 'Ethan Allen' class, were designed specifically from the beginning for the fleet ballistic

missile deterrent role. They are considerably larger and somewhat better arranged as regards layout than the earlier SSBNs of the 'George Washington' class. With a submerged displacement of 7,900 tons, that is heavier by 1,200 tons, they have an overall length extended to 410.5ft, a beam of 33ft and a draught of 30ft; but they have only four torpedo tubes. Otherwise, as regards the main propelling machinery and the crew particulars, they are practically identical.

The *Ethan Allen* and *Thomas A. Edison* were constructed by General Dynamics (Electric Boat) while the *Sam Houston, John Marshall* and *Thomas Jefferson* were built by the Newport News Shipbuilding & DD Company. All five ships were laid down between 1959 and 1961 and completed in an average time of two years from 1961 to 1963. They were initially armed with the POLARIS A-2 ballistic missiles with a range of 1,725 statute miles, but all five of these bigger

The American carrier *Enterprise* was the world's second nuclear powered warship; she is also the world's largest warship (89,600 tons), but will be exceeded in displacement by the 'Nimitz' class when they are completed.

SSBNs are being modified to fire the longer range A-3 missiles.

About this time, with the perfection of the nuclear powered fleet ballistic missile submarine, the United States Navy decided to embark on series building of such a numerically large class of uniform design that it amounted to practically mass production of SSBNs on homogeneous lines, and the prototype of this even bigger class dimensionally, the USS *Lafayette*, SSBN 616, became the first of the eventual 31 vessels which were the largest underwater craft ever built. Their construction was shared by General Dynamics Electric Boat Division, Mare Island Naval Shipyard, Portsmouth Naval Shipyard, and Newport News Shipbuilding & DD Co, only four yards for such a larger number of submarines of immense size and complexity, ensuring an economy of pipeline and production methods, and obviating a proliferation of drawing and work schedules.

All of these 31 submarines, both nuclear powered and ballistic missile armed, and now by general consent promoted from the old and traditional designation of 'boats' to the new and more fitting status of 'ships', were laid down between 1961 and 1965 and completed during 1963 to 1967, a quite astonishing shipbuilding feat, especially in such a highly specialised field of technical, engineering, and scientific complexity, and a most creditable performance, which probably could only have been accomplished at the time in the United States alone, of all the nations in the western world.

The 'Lafayette' class of SSBNs have a submerged displacement of 8,250 tons with an overall length of 425ft, a beam of 33.2ft and a draught of 31.5ft. The power plant and associated machinery is much the same as in the earlier classes of nuclear powered fleet ballistic missile armed submarines, except that the *Benjamin Franklin*, SSBN 640, the twentieth ship of the class and later vessels of the group, which pedantically are officially considered to be a sub-class in a separate list, have quieter machinery. The personnel complement was increased to 140, comprising 14 officers and 126 enlisted men, with two complete ship's companies for each submarine, alternating in 'Blue' and 'Gold' watches, each of which undertakes a patrol of sixty days duration followed by a spell of 28 days refitting, while the off-duty crew is on leave or undergoing training courses.

The first eight ships of the 'Lafayette' class were equipped with POLARIS A-2 ballistic missiles and the 23 later vessels with the POLARIS A-3 missiles. Five of the earlier ships were re-armed with the A-3 missiles between 1968 and 1970. It is planned to convert these ships to carry the new POSEIDON fleet ballistic missile system. The first of the class to undergo POSEIDON conversion was the *James Madison* from 1969 to 1970, and the conversion schedule for twenty ships should be completed by 1976 or 1977. All the SSBNs of the 'Lafayette' class are also armed with four 21in torpedo tubes.

So altogether the United States Navy has a strategic warfare force, or nuclear deterrent,

The nuclear powered guided missile cruiser *Long Beach* 17,360 tons, was the first nuclear powered warship in the world, and the first to mount guided missiles instead of guns for a main battery.

16

of 41 POLARIS-POSEIDON submarines carrying no fewer than 656 fleet ballistic missiles.

While the United States had been thus occupied in getting to such an advanced stage, however, Russia, where the world's first nuclear powered surface ship, the giant icebreaker *Lenin*, of 16,000 tons displacement with three nuclear reactors, had been launched in 1957, had been far from idle in the field of nuclear powered submarine development, and Soviet engineers and naval architects and scientists worked rapidly on hulls, propelling machinery and rockets.

From the prototype Soviet nuclear powered submarine there developed a production class of fourteen vessels (one was lost) of the so-called 'N' class. Built between 1958 and 1965,

they were designed for fleet duties and anti-submarine warfare and were armed with torpedo tubes. These were followed by seven vessels of the 'V' class built from 1968 onwards, which were nuclear powered, but otherwise had conventional submarine propensities.

From 1961 onwards the Soviet Navy built four long range nuclear powered submarines of the 'E 1' class armed with six SHADDOCK cruise missile tubes as well as ten torpedo tubes; and these were succeeded by 27 nuclear powered cruise missile submarines of the 'E 2' class built from 1962 onwards, which have eight SHADDOCK missile tubes with ten torpedo tubes. The five nuclear powered cruise missile submarines of the 'C' class built since about

The nuclear powered guided missile frigate *Truxton* has a displacement of 9,200 tons and is armed with a dual purpose 'Terrier/Asroc' launcher aft as well

as one 5-inch, two 3-inch and four fixed Mk 32 torpedo launchers.

The Russian missile cruiser helicopter carrier
Moskva, built at Nikolaev in the Black Sea, where
there are now indications that a large vessel of
about 30,000 tons (possibly an aircraft carrier) is
under construction.

1968 have eight tubes for surface-to-surface
missiles as well as eight torpedo tubes.

In the meantime the first Soviet nuclear
powered ballistic missile armed submarines,
the group comprising the 'H 1' and 'H 2'
classes, had been developed practically on
parallel lines with the original nuclear powered
submarines of the 'N' class. This 'H' group,
built from about 1961 onwards, have three
SSN5 ballistic missile tubes as well as ten
torpedo tubes.

Until recent years all Soviet nuclear powered
submarines, whether standard submarines,
cruise missile submarines or ballistic missile
submarines, had an average displacement of
about 5,000 tons, but with the advent of the
much larger United States deterrent submarines, and the necessity to mount many
more vertical tubes, there was a big leap in the

size of the next class of Soviet deterrent
submarines.

The eighteen nuclear powered ballistic
missile submarines of the 'Y' class have a
displacement of about 9,000 tons submerged
and are armed with sixteen SAWFLY missile
tubes as well as eight torpedo tubes. These
vessels are, of course, comparable with, and
equivalent to, the largest fleet ballistic missile
armed nuclear powered submarines in the
United States Navy.

In addition to nuclear powered submarines
armed with ballistic missile tubes and cruise
missile tubes, the Soviet Navy also has conventionally powered submarines armed with
long range, medium range and short range
missiles. These comprise 22 submarines of the
'G' class mounting three SSN5 ballistic missile
tubes, four more submarines of the 'Z 5'

class with two SSN4 ballistic missile tubes, sixteen modern submarines of the 'J' class with four SHADDOCK cruise missile tubes, six 'Long Bin' type submarines of the 'W' class with four SHADDOCK cruise missile tubes, and six 'Twin Cylinder' type submarines of the 'W' class carrying two SHADDOCK cruise missile launchers.

The first British nuclear powered submarine was HMS *Dreadnought* of 4,000 tons displacement, armed with six 21in torpedo tubes, which was laid down by Vickers Limited Shipbuilding Group, Barrow-in-Furness in June 1959, and commissioned in April 1963.

This prototype of the Royal Navy's 'fleet' or hunter-killer nuclear powered submarines was followed by a production series, the five vessels of the 'Valiant' class, namely HMS *Churchill*, *Conqueror*, *Courageous*, *Valiant* and *Warspite*, of 4,500 tons, all completed between 1966 and 1971, all by Vickers, except

Conqueror by Cammell Laird & Co Ltd, Birkenhead.

Four improved nuclear powered fleet submarines of the 'Swiftsure' class, those named at the time of going to press being *Sovereign*, *Superb* and *Swiftsure*, are under construction by Vickers.

After the first two submarines of the 'Valiant' class, namely *Valiant* and *Warspite*, had been completed, the construction of British nuclear powered fleet submarines was by official policy deliberately slowed down, in order that priority could be given to the Royal Navy's first construction of nuclear powered ballistic missile armed submarines.

Accordingly the four SSBNs of the 'R' class were all built in a comparatively short period, having been laid down in 1964 and 1965 and completed between 1967 and 1969, the *Renown* and *Revenge* by Cammell Laird and the *Repulse* and *Resolution* by Vickers.

A dual purpose anti-submarine/guided missile armed destroyer of the 'Kresta I' class.

All four of these much larger nuclear powered submarines have a submerged displacement of 8,400 tons and are armed with sixteen POLARIS A-3 ballistic missile tubes with a range of 2,880 miles, as well as six 21in torpedo tubes. Each ship has two crews of 141, comprising 13 officers and 128 ratings, who relieve each other approximately every three months in order to get maximum operation time at sea.

In the French Navy *Le Redoutable* was the first nuclear powered submarine and also the first nuclear powered ballistic missile submarine, but she was not the first ballistic missile submarine, for France developed her submarine deterrent in a different way.

The *Gymnote* is a conventionally powered submarine but fitted with four tubes for ballistic missiles. Laid down in 1963 and completed in 1966, she has a submerged displacement of 3,250 tons. She was originally the hull of what was intended to be a nuclear powered submarine laid down in 1958, but cancelled in 1959. Built by Cherbourg Naval Dockyard, she is used as a test vehicle for trials and experiments with ballistic missiles for the first French deterrent submarines, and as a laboratory to prove equipment for them.

Le Redoutable is the prototype of the French *Force de dissuasion* of four or five such vessels which the Navy plans to have in the late 1970s. Laid down in March 1964 and launched in March 1967, she started trials in 1969 and became officially operational on December 1st, 1971. Her sister ship *Le Terrible*, laid down in June 1967 and launched in December 1969, is on trials. The third French nuclear powered ballistic missile armed submarine, *Le Foudroyant*, laid down in 1969, was launched on December 4th, 1971. And the fourth of this class of big deterrent submarines specifically built as strategic warfare ships, *L'Indomptable*, was started at the end of 1971. The construction of all four was undertaken by Cherbourg Naval Dockyard.

Practically similar in most respects to the United States deterrent submarines of the 'Lafayette' class and the British POLARIS armed submarines of the 'Resolution' class, the French nuclear powered ballistic missile submarines of the 'Le Redoutable' class have a submerged displacement of about 9,000 tons with a length of 420ft, a beam of 34.8ft and a draught of 32.8ft.

It will be seen from the above brief look at the actual floating hardware that the possible antagonists in the field of strategic warfare as manifested by deterrent submarines are evenly, or delicately balanced.

But the four major naval powers have to look not only to an inconceivable use of the nuclear deterrent, but to a viable deterrent for peace-time, cold war, or extreme measures short of all-out nuclear war.

And since the great battleships, the ultimate development of big-gun armament, became obsolete, the standard deterrent has been the new capital ship in the shape of fixed-wing aircraft carriers, in which the gun mounting has been replaced by the catapult, and the shell by a man-guided flying projectile (the present sophisticated naval strike aircraft) giving a vast extension of the shell's range.

These capital ships are augmented or supported by guided missile armed destroyers, frigates and amphibious ships, which within the scope of a comparatively short article covering a survey of such wide compass, the following is merely a summary.

The United States Navy has fifteen front-line fixed-wing aircraft carriers, known as Attack Carriers, CVA. These include the USS *Enterprise*, CVAN 65, a nuclear powered colossus of 89,600 tons full load displacement with an overall length of 1,123ft and a maximum width of 257ft, the largest warship ever built at the time of her construction, having been laid down in February 1958 and complated in November 1961, a remarkably short time for a ship of her massive dimensions and complexity. She can carry more than ninety aircraft, and is equipped with four steam catapults to launch them. She is armed with two Basic Point Defence Missile System (BPDMS) launchers with SEA SPARROW missiles. Her propelling machinery plant consists of eight Westinghouse A2W pressurised water-cooled nuclear reactors and four

HMS *Eagle*, 50,800 tons, July 1969. Underwent extensive reconstruction and modernisation between 1959 and 1964, and again in 1966–67, when she was equipped to operate Phantom aircraft.

[*MoD, RN, Official*

HMS *London* one of the eight British 'County' class guided missile armed destroyers. Armed with four 4.5-inch, two 20mm, one 'Seaslug' guided missile launcher, two quadruple 'Seacat' launchers and two sextuple 3-inch flare launchers and a 'Wessex' anti-submarine helicopter.

[*MoD, RN, Official*

sets of geared steam turbines turning four shafts and developing some 280,000 shaft horse power and equal to a speed of 35 knots. She has a total complement of no fewer than 5,500, comprising 3,100 as the ship's company (162 officers and 2,938 enlisted men) plus 2,400 assigned to the attack air wing.

Newport News, who built the *Enterprise*, also have under construction two more nuclear powered aircraft carriers, the *Nimitz*, CVAN 68, and the *Dwight D. Eisenhower*, CVAN 69, both even heavier ships, with a full load displacement of 95,100 tons.

The other fourteen existing aircraft carriers are: Four of the 'Kitty Hawk' class, the *Kitty Hawk*, CVA 63, *Constellation*, CVA 64, *America*, CVA 66, and *John F. Kennedy*, CVA 67, of 80,800 to 87,000 tons full load displacement and carrying 80 to 90 aircraft, the ships being propelled by high pressure boilers and geared turbines and armed with missiles, all commissioned between 1961 and 1968; Four of the 'Forrestal' class, the *Forrestal*, CVA 59, *Saratoga*, CVA 60, *Ranger*, CVA 61, and *Independence*, CVA 62, also conventionally powered with a displacement of 78,000 tons full load, and a capacity of eighty aircraft, all commissioned from 1955 –1959; Three of the 'Midway' class, the *Midway*, CVA 41, *Franklin D. Roosevelt*, CVA 42, and *Coral Sea*, CVA 43, with displacements of approximately 64,000 tons full load, a complement of 75 aircraft and orthodox propelling machinery, first commissioned between 1945 and 1947, but regularly updated ever since; the three of the 'Hancock' (Modified 'Essex') class, the *Hancock*, CVA 19, *Bon Homme Richard*, CVA 31, and *Oriskany*, CVA 34, all of about 44,700 tons full load displacement with conventional engineering plant and carrying 70 to 80 aircraft, of which the first two were completed in 1944, but have been extensively modernised (now decommissioned) and *Oriskany* to a later design in 1950.

In addition to these front-line aircraft carriers the United States Navy has a dozen other aircraft carriers of the 'Essex' class of military value almost equal to the 'Han-

cock' class above. All of from 38,000 to 41,730 tons full load displacement, eleven are designated ASW (Anti-Submarine Warfare) Support Aircraft Carriers, CVS, and *Lexington* as Training Aircraft Carrier (CVT). These ships carry 40 to 50 aircraft, of which two-fifths are helicopters, and are armed with the reduced armament of four 5in guns now normal in the war-built, and first post-war aircraft carriers. All were first commissioned between 1942 and 1946, but eight are now in reserve.

The United States Navy also operates a very useful class of seven other flat-tops, the 'Iwo Jima' class, officially rated as Amphibious Assault Ships and designated LPH. The *Iwo Jima*, *Okinawa*, *Guadalcanal*, *Guam*, *Tripoli*, *New Oreans* and *Inchon*, with a full load displacement of 18,300 tons, each carry 28 to 32 helicopters and are armed with eight 3in guns (six in *Okinawa* which has a BPDMS launcher for SEA SPARROW Missiles). This class of ship was the first in the world designed and constructed specifically to operate helicopters. They were completed from 1961 to 1970.

(There are also seven aircraft ferry ships designated AKV, former escort aircraft carriers, *Card*, *Core*, *Croatan* and *Breton* of the 'Bogue' class, displacing 15,700 tons full load, which originally carried thirty aircraft, built in 1942 and 1943; and *Kula Gulf*, *Point Cruz* and *Rabaul* of the 'Commencement Bay' class, of 24,275 tons full load displacement, with a capacity of 34 aircraft as designed, built in 1945 and 1946. All are in reserve.)

Amphibious warfare ships in the United States Navy also include fifteen half flat-tops, known as amphibious transports dock (LPD), capable of carrying six helicopters operated from the flight deck aft, and telescopic hangars amidships. The twelve ships of the 'Austin' class completed between 1965 and 1971 displace 16,900 tons full load, and the three forerunners of the 'Raleigh' class commissioned from 1962 to 1964 came out at 13,900 tons full load. The two dozen dock landing ships (LSD), comprising five of the 'Anchorage' class, 13,650 tons full load, built between

1969 and 1972, eight of the 'Thomaston' class, 11,270 to 12,150 tons full load, built between 1954 and 1957, and eleven of the 'Casa Grande' class, 9,375 to 10,000 tons, built between 1944 and 1946, are all fitted with helicopter landing decks aft.

To return from the air sphere to the submarine field for a moment, it is not generally realised that the United States Navy recently completed its 100th nuclear powered submarine. Of the hundred, 41 are deterrent submarines, and the remainder attack or fleet submarines. But there are now only fifty diesel powered submarines in the American Navy, compared with the 200-odd of a decade or so ago, and of these only a dozen are post-war boats, the remainder having been war-built.

Apart from carriers of all categories and submarines of all types summarised in the foregoing, the main bulk of the United States Navy is constituted by what are now known as surface combatants and ocean escorts, which together run into 462 ships, of which 257 are active, and the remainder in reserve. But there are also 26 fighting ships, all except one in reserve, including the powerful categories of battleships and heavy cruisers, which in former days formed the backbone of the Navy, now known as 'Fire Support Ships'.

The surface combatants comprise:— ten guided missile cruisers including the nuclear powered *Long Beach* of 17,360 tons full load displacement, the turbine powered *Albany*, *Chicago* and *Columbus*, each displacing 17,500 tons full load, and the so-called 'light' cruisers of the converted 'Cleveland' class, *Little Rock*, *Oklahoma City*, *Providence*, *Springfield*, *Galveston* and *Topeka*, of 14,600 tons full load, of which the latter two are in reserve, also conventionally powered.

Thirty-three so-called 'frigates' comprising the nuclear powered *Truxtun* and *Bainbridge*, of 9,200 and 8,580 tons full load respectively (as big as cruisers), and armed with missiles as well as guns; 28 guided missile frigates of three groups, the nine of the 'Belknap' class of 7,930 tons full load, nine of the 'Leahy'

class displacing 7,800 tons full load, and ten of the 'Coontz' class, 5800 tons full load; two all-gun frigates of the 'Mitscher' class (the original 'destroyer leaders') of 4,730 tons full load, and the all-gun frigate *Norfolk* (originally a light cruiser 'killer' for anti-submarine warfare), of 7,300 tons full load, all three of the latter being in reserve.

And 232 destroyers comprising 29 missile armed ships—two of the 'Mitscher' class, 5,155 tons full load, four of the converted 'Forrest Sherman' class, 4,105 tons full load, and 23 of the 'Charles F. Adams' class, 4,500 tons; and 203 conventional all-gun destroyers, fourteen of these being post-war vessels of the 'Forrest Sherman' class, and 189 orthodox destroyers built during World War II of 3,050 to 3,520 tons full load of the 'Gearing', 'Allen M. Summer' and 'Fletcher' classes and variations, 76 of which are laid up in reserve.

The ocean escorts (formerly known as destroyer escorts) comprise six missile escort ships of the 'Brooke' class, 3,425 tons full load; 55 post-war all-gun escort ships including 25 of the 'Knox' class, 4,100 tons, ten of the 'Garcia' class, 3,400 tons, two of the 'Bronstein' class, 2,650 tons, four of the 'Claud Jones' class, 1750 tons, and thirteen of the 'Dealey' group, 1,914 tons; and 126 war-built escort ships of 1,850 to 2,230 tons, all laid up in reserve except two.

The 'Fire Support Ships' (which except for the few remaining rocket ships means outmoded capital ships and all-big-gun ships) comprises four battleships of 59,000 tons full load displacement with a main armament of nine 16in guns completed in 1943–1944, namely the *Iowa*, *Missouri*, *New Jersey* and *Wisconsin*, relics of the great deterrent forces of the past; the missile and gun armed heavy cruisers *Boston* and *Canberra* of 17,700 tons full load completed in 1943 and converted in 1955–1956; the heavy cruisers *Des Moines*, *Newport News* and *Salem* of 21,500 tons full load completed in 1948 and 1949; the heavy cruiser *Rochester* of 17,500 tons full load first commissioned in 1946; and seven heavy cruisers of the ('Baltimore') class, 17,200 tons, completed in 1943–1946. The others are eight small ships of 1,084 tons full load, war-built rocket landing ships of the 'River' class now known as inshore fire support ships, and the post-war *Carronade* of 1,500 tons completed in 1955.

The remaining, but by no means unimportant, proportion of the American Fleet, which can only be barely listed here in an article of limited length, comprises:— Two command ships (the converted aircraft carrier *Wright* of 19,600 tons and the converted heavy cruiser *Northampton* of 17,200 tons), two communications ships (the converted aircraft carrier *Arlington* (ex-*Saipan*), of 19,600 tons and the modified escort carrier *Annapolis* (ex-*Gilbert Islands*), of 22,500 tons full load), all four in reserve, and the flagship (small seaplane tender) *Valcour* of 2,800 tons.

Seven amphibious command ships (two new of 19,290 tons and five war-built of 12,560 tons of which four are in reserve), nineteen amphibious cargo ships (six active), 13 amphibious transports (three active), eleven small amphibious transports (former destroyer escorts, all in reserve), 58 tank landing ships (31 in reserve), seventeen patrol gunboats, four hydrofoils, eighteen fast patrol craft, 51 ocean minesweepers (nineteen in reserve), 29 war-built fleet mine-sweepers (all in reserve), fourteen coastal minesweepers, 82 replenishment ships (twenty in reserve), 152 fleet support ships (63 in reserve), 101 logistic support ships, 45 surveying and research ships, and a large number of auxiliaries, landing craft, river craft and service craft. The Fleet Train, of course, represents a large part of United States sea power as a back-up to the combatant ships constituting the peace-time or cold war deterrent.

Increasingly in recent years the Soviet Union has also realised the military and prestige value of global sea power from both strategic and tactical purpose ships. In addition to the ninety nuclear powered submarines outlined earlier, Russia has some 320 conventionally powered submarines mainly built in standardised batches and numerically large classes, mostly of the fleet type, but many armed with missiles, from series design and production, the basic post-war 'W' group and variations running into 170 units.

Of great interest to the western powers are the two Soviet CGHs or missile cruiser helicopter carriers *Leningrad* and *Moskva*, of 18,000 tons full load displacement, bristling with guided missiles and directors tiered on the forward half of the ship and equipped with hangar and flight deck in the after half of the ship to carry up to twenty normal and thirty maximum helicopters. These ships could of course operate V/STOL aircraft.

Although they were officially considered to be outmoded some years ago the Soviet Union still has a dozen post-war orthodox cruisers of 19,200 tons, the 'Sverdlov' class, but she has as many missile cruisers of the "Kresta II". 'Kresta I' and 'Kynda' classes ranging from 6,000 to 7,500 tons built in recent years, and three dozen other rocket ships or missile destroyers of the 'Krivak', 'Kashin', 'Kanin', 'Krupny', 'Kotlin SAM' and 'Kildin' classes ranging from 3,885 to 5,200 tons. There are also some seventy conventionally armed destroyers of the 'Kotlin' and 'Skory' classes and about 130 smaller escort ships of the small frigate and corvette types, the 'Nanuchka', 'Mirka', 'Petya', 'Kola' and 'Riga' classes.

The Soviet Navy also maintains a score of large fleet support ships, some 270 coastal escorts and patrol vessels, about 320 fleet, coastal and inshore minesweepers, no fewer than 125 fast missile boats, as many as 325 fast torpedo boats, about 130 amphibious ships, and some 75 landing craft, excluding ship-borne units. Specialised support ships, auxiliary vessels, intelligence trawlers, surveying vessels, research ships and service craft run into several thousands.

An important consideration is that the bulk of the Soviet Fleet has been built since World War II. Most ships are of recent construction. Not many ships are out of commission. Most modern ships not being routine refitted are fully manned and operational, but some of the older ships are in reserve. Several categories of warships, including cruisers, destroyers, submarines and many smaller craft are

French aircraft carrier *Foch*, 32,800 tons. Carries a total of 30 aircraft.   *[French Navy, Official*

fitted for minelaying, which has always been a highly specialised branch of the Soviet Navy, and the fleet is therefore capable of a considerable minelaying effort. Some classes of otherwise conventional ships are fitted with missiles.

Until recently Great Britain had five fixed wing aircraft carriers, but *Victorious* was scrapped, *Centaur* was discarded as an accommodation ship, and *Hermes* was relegated to a commando ship, leaving only

Ark Royal and *Eagle*, each of 50,800 tons full load displacement, in commission, but the latter ship's days are numbered, despite the fact that she completed reconstruction and modernisation in 1964 at a cost of £31 million. The Fleet Air Arm is only viable of course with an absolute minimum of two aircraft carriers, for to keep one fixed wing aircraft carrier operational at all times a sister ship is required as a back-up relief carrier in case of damage by action, collision,

25

explosion, grounding, hurricane or any other hazard, or while she is being routine refitted in dockyard.

The Royal Navy's amphibious ships include the commando ships *Albion* and *Bulwark* of 27,700 tons (one to be relieved by *Hermes*), the assault ships *Fearless* and *Intrepid* of 12,120 tons, and the command helicopter cruisers *Blake* and *Tiger* of 12,080 tons. There are also six logistic landing ships of the 'Knight' class, 5,700 tons, operated as Royal Fleet Auxiliaries.

In addition to the four deterrent submarines of the 'R' class and six other nuclear powered (fleet) submarines of the hunter-killer types mentioned earlier, there are 21 conventionally powered post-war built patrol submarines of the 'Oberon' and 'Porpoise' classes, of 2,410 tons submerged displacement.

The United Kingdom also has nine guided missile armed destroyers, 65 frigates, 49 coastal minesweepers and minehunters, 54 fleet support ships, and 390 inshore vessels, landing craft, training boats, mooring vessels, fleet tenders, auxiliaries and tugs.

The Fleet Air Arm in the French Navy is represented by the fixed wing aircraft carriers *Clemenceau* and *Foch* of 32,800 tons, the helicopter carrier *Arromanches* (ex-British *Colossus*) of 18,500 tons, and the helicopter carrier cruiser *Jeanne d'Arc* of 12,360 tons.

In addition to the missile submarines for strategic warfare summarised in the first part of this survey, the French Navy also maintains nineteen diesel and electric powered submarines, comprising six ocean going vessels of the 'Narval' class with a submerged displacement of 1,910 tons, nine medium units of the 'Daphne' class with a submerged displacement averaging 1,050 tons, and four coastal boats displacing 670 tons submerged, all being of post-war design and construction.

France also has an anti-aircraft missile cruiser, a command ship converted from a cruiser, three guided missile armed frigates, four guided missile armed destroyers, thirteen other destroyers, 27 frigates, fourteen ocean minesweepers, 62 coastal minesweepers and minehunters, fifteen inshore minesweepers, fifteen patrol vessels, and 160 fleet support ships, experimental vessels, maintenance ships, survey vessels, logistic ships, landing vessels and service craft.

From the foregoing digest of the present state of the four major powers having a nuclear deterrent and the comparison of their basic naval strengths in hardware alone, it will be observed that certain trends have emerged.

A large proportion of the United States Fleet is of wartime construction and is laid up in reserve.

The large majority of the ships in the Soviet Navy are of post war construction and are nearly all active.

The bigger ships of the Royal Navy are still being reduced, and the Fleet now largely comprises small vessels.

The French Navy is being neither unduly expanded nor reduced, and is preserving a nice balance of warship categories.

The Royal Navy in the Seventies

DESMOND WETTERN

Naval correspondent of the *Sunday Telegraph*

The next half decade is likely to be, and indeed is already showing signs of being, one of the most transitional in the Royal Navy for at least a century. Not only is the weaponry changing but so, too, is the entire strategic concept of the Navy's role.

The kind of weapons and the strategy under which the Navy is deployed do not, unfortunately, by any means match, and today the Service is increasingly being placed, for that of a major maritime power anyway, in the unenviable position in which the weaponry 'tail' wags the strategic 'dog'.

Four years ago the position was clear enough: the Navy was to become essentially a North Atlantic one largely tailored to meet NATO requirements. The world-wide 'policing' role, albeit declining over the preceding twenty years, was finally to be a thing of the past.

Such a policy to many had the merit of realism. The Fleet *was* too small to keep up the 'pretence' of a world-wide capability any longer. Moreover, the main threat stemmed from the expanding Soviet Navy, particularly in far northern waters.

It therefore seemed logical that the Navy's main strength should be concentrated in northern European waters. In addition, to find the money for a fleet that would make a worthwhile contribution to the NATO forces might at least be within bounds of economic possibility and political expediency.

There were, too, a number of 'fringe' benefits. A largely home-based Navy would reduce separation from wives and families—always a disincentive to re-engagement—and there would no longer be the political, foreign exchange and security problems that may arise with bases overseas.

But this neat and tidy 'package' that Labour Defence Minister Denis Healey had in mind had one basic flaw: seapower cannot be boxed up into politically convenient and economically manageable units—in other words 'seapower is not divisible'. Even senior NATO naval commanders admit that the geographical limitations placed upon the Alliance, at sea at least, would rapidly become meaningless in time of war or major emergency. So long as Britain continues to have the largest active mercantile marine in the world and has investment and trading interests on a *world-wide scale* no amount of waving of politicians' magic wands will make the commitments for which we have a Navy disappear.

It does no harm to restate what some of these commitments are: that 95 per cent of our trade, notably oil and raw materials, is carried by ships; that without the free access of ships to these islands all other factors such as our political influence upon world affairs; our economic position and—ultimately—our survival must be set at nought.

Mr Healey's argument was that the threat lay in waters nearest home, and certainly the North Sea and the North Atlantic are major areas of Soviet naval activity with the Mediterranean coming a close second. Yet one of the classic advantages of a fleet is its mobility. Just as we have tried to prune costs by concentrating the Navy in home waters so the Soviet Navy is all too well aware that for some time at least logistic problems will also hamper their deployment of large squadrons East of Suez. But it would be foolish to believe that they could not, if the political goal was worthwhile, deploy considerable naval forces outside the North Atlantic and Mediterranean—indeed there are already signs that their scale of activity in the Indian Ocean and South Atlantic is increasing.

Following the 1970 General Election the new government decided on a course of compromise as it saw it. The bulk of the Fleet, in accordance with the Healey doctrine, would be concentrated in home waters but a

HMS Amazon, the first of the Type 21 frigates ordered by the Navy being launched at the Woolston yard of Vosper-Thornycroft on April 26, 1971. A further seven vessels of this type are under construction.

[MoD, RN, Official

Singapore—Britain's last major overseas base where a toehold is still retained under the ANZUK command. A Royal Fleet Auxiliary is seen here under repair in one of the five floating docks.

[Desmond Wettern

force of six destroyers or frigates would remain East of Suez.

As Mr Healey had done, there were assurances that this force could be rapidly reinforced in the event of emergency. But it is at this point that the problem for the Navy's planners arose.

If the Navy was still to be capable, even if largely not so deployed, of carrying out tasks around the world rather than within the confines of the North Atlantic Alliance there would be grave difficulties in matching this potential commitment with a Navy whose strategic role would be containment, rather, perhaps a contribution toward containment, of the Soviet Northern Fleet.

A Navy geared towards a policy of contain-

ment would require a high degree of sophistication. Quality rather than quantity would be essential. But if, at the same time, these same ships might also have to patrol the Persian Gulf or mount some new Beira blockade then a number of other factors, not always compatible with those for a 'North Atlantic Navy', would have to be considered. For example, electronics systems and weaponry might have to be just that much less complex and sophisticated bearing in mind that a ship might have to operate independently thousands of miles from the nearest dockyard and perhaps even in a situation where there might be problems flying in one of the ubiquitous Fleet Maintenance Units. Habitability would be of greater importance than in ships which might not spend more than a couple of weeks at sea at a stretch.

One can, perhaps, see a reflection of the planners' problems in the face of changing commitments with the new Type 21 frigate design. As originally conceived these ships, utilising commercial yards' design features, were to be 'stopgaps' between the 'Leander' class and the new Type 22 in the design stage. They would be cheaper than, or certainly as cheap as, the 'Leander' class. In some quarters it was thought that the Navy was at last producing a kind of latterday 'gunboat' designed with an East of Suez role in mind.

But what will finally emerge? Ships costing between £8 million and £10 million each which, with systems like Computer-Assisted Action Information System (CAAIS), will be even more complex than the 'Leander' class. So, too, with the Type 42 missile destroyers. These were to be cut-down Type 82s probably somewhat less expensive than the later County class units. But *Sheffield*, the first, will cost £17 million, about £2 million more than the Counties, and £7 million more than the one, and only, Type 82 HMS *Bristol* was planned to cost back in the 'sixties.

Inevitably, such costly ships will never be provided in the numbers that would enable any government to deploy sizeable forces East of Suez and at the same time maintain a 'meaningful' contribution within NATO. So, the weaponry will increasingly force upon any government the choice between the East of Suez or the NATO commitment.

Britain, aspiring to join the Common Market—virtually within it already in fact—and worried by the threat of a declining American contribution to NATO, cannot but choose to have a Navy orientated toward the meeting of the NATO commitment, the politicians argue, but such is the sophistication and cost of new ships now in the pipeline she could not do otherwise.

But the big question is whether the Navy of the next decade, as now envisaged, matches this choice. Here there must be grave reservations.

Inevitably, any warship's design is a compromise between the various staff requirements. These requirements, basically, cover: armament, speed, endurance, sea-keeping, habitability, ease of maintenance and repair—all set within a cost ceiling.

Obviously, all those factors must be looked at in the light of the potential threat and the tasks it is envisaged the ship should perform.

There are many who would argue that the greatest threat lies East of Suez in that in the West the use of nuclear weapons after only a few days fighting with conventional weapons places the stakes too high for the Kremlin to start any armed escapades. Rightly or wrongly both the major political parties in Britain do not accept this and believe that the greatest threat to the Western allies lies on their own doorsteps. Expressed more honestly perhaps, what this implies is that as we cannot afford to maintain an East of Suez presence to any great extent as well as making a contribution to NATO so, as pointed out earlier, we opt for the more politically expedient and economically less onerous although possibly less real commitment.

That being the case, what is the threat to NATO at sea? By 1975 at the latest Russia will have more nuclear submarines—by about 50 to 75 boats—than all three of the Western nuclear powers combined. These boats include ballistic missile, tactical missile, Fleet (or hunter-killer) and conventional patrol types. Somewhat surprisingly, Russia unlike Britain or America is continuing to build diesel-electric patrol type submarines—but she is also building between four and five nuclear boats a month as well; so those who sought consolation in the continuing Soviet diesel-electric submarine programme being indicative of a tapering off of their nuclear submarine programme will be disappointed.

The ballistic missile submarines need not be considered except briefly. They belong to the realm of the nuclear exchange at which point relative naval capabilities become meaningless. Until there is, or if there is, a major breakthrough in underwater detection systems some of these submarines would always be able to launch their missiles no

A 'Sea King' helicopter hovers above parked 'Phantoms' on the flight deck of *Ark Royal*. The 'Sea King' has equipment comparable to that in a small frigate. *[MoD, RN, Official*

matter how vast the West's anti-submarine forces might be.

The tactical missile firing submarine, whether nuclear or conventional, has two weak spots. Beyond a distance of around 20–25 miles (or the launching ship's own radar horizon) the missile would have to be guided to its target—or at least 'pointed in the right direction'—by some mid-course guidance vehicle such as an aircraft feeding in coordinates to the point where the local guidance system within the missile took over. This might be by infra-red heat-seeking sensors or perhaps television. (STYX used against the Israeli destroyer *Eilath* in 1967 is an example of the former while the air-to-surface MARTEL is an example of the latter). The missile submarine's second weak spot is that for about three minutes part of it must surface to launch its missiles.

So, defending naval forces must have the means to destroy quickly and at long range the guidance aircraft. They may also, of course, try to destroy the submarine in the three minutes part of it is above water, but this pre-supposes that there is an indication that the submarine is in the area. To achieve a level of surveillance that would make this possible, even in quite a small sea area, would require round-the-clock all-weather air patrols calling for far greater numbers of aircraft than are likely to be available to NATO, let alone Britain, for years, if at all.

The Soviet surface threat lies mainly with its missile cruisers and destroyers. Again, missiles like SHADDOCK, the surface-to-surface system fitted in the 'Kresta' I and II class missile cruisers, must have some mid-course guidance unless launched within the comparatively short range of the ship's own radar—say twenty miles.

How, then, is the Royal Navy likely to be

able to meet such threats in the next few years?

By the mid-seventies there will be ten nuclear Fleet submarines in service. Although twenty by 1980 was the aim some years ago it seems most unlikely that by that time we shall have achieved 75 per cent of that goal. These ships have extremely powerful Sonar because of the tremendous generator capacity conferred by their power source, but it must be borne in mind that employed 'actively' Sonar cannot be used with much hope of success in a surprise attack. Certainly, work in connection with improving the direction-finding capability of Sonar used in the 'passive' or simple hydrophonic mode is going ahead, but really accurate D/F with 'passive' Sonar is probably some way off.

Then, too, the nuclear Fleet submarine has great speed and endurance. But so, too, do Russian nuclear tactical missile submarines.

Against surface targets our Fleet submarines must for some time to come rely upon torpedoes with a likely effective range of around four miles. Trials are going ahead with SLAM, an adaptation of BLOWPIPE, against helicopters and small patrol craft such as hovercraft, but the Navy is lukewarm on the SLAM project. There is therefore an urgent need for a longer range underwater-launched missile system that can be used against surface targets. One

such project was cancelled in 1968–69 and despite constant urging by successive Flag Officers Submarines neither this government nor its predecessors show any inclination to give the green light to the project's development—even though it is well within the Navy's and industry's research and development capabilities.

Certainly, the anti-submarine armoury in our Fleet submarines is being enhanced with wire-guided torpedoes but the present armament for use against surface targets has been likened to 'putting a spear in a Chieftain tank'.

The diesel-electric 'Oberon' and 'Porpoise' class submarines, which will be with us until the early 1980s, have the same weapon limitations but lack the Fleet submarines' Sonar. Suggestions that we might revert to building patrol type submarines are officially unacceptable on the grounds that with a limited budget it would be wrong not to build the best possible submarines. Once again, we see the 'quality versus quantity' factor.

Turning to surface ships; the County class missile destroyers have been cursed with electronic and marine engineering problems. Four have a limited surface-to-surface missile system with SEASLUG II and the earlier four will not now be converted to use this missile. If they were able to get within radar guidance range and enemy Electronic Counter Mea-

A 'Nimrod' of RAF Strike Command, seen from HMS Rapid, overflying Keppel (left); Wave Chief and Cavalier (right); shortly before the start of Exercise 'HIGHWOOD' in the North Sea in December 1971.
[Desmond Wettern

The guided missile destroyers *Norfolk*, nearest the camera, *London* and *Antrim* in company after the maritime air defence exercise 'HIGHWOOD' in December 1971. All three ships were 'sunk' or 'damaged' by elderly ships playing the roles of Russian missile ships during the exercise.

[MoD, RN, Official

sures (ECM) jamming could be prevented or avoided no doubt these ships could give a fair account of themselves—but these are big 'ifs'. In due course they will probably be refitted to take the Sea King helicopter which is a first class anti-submarine weapon system with the combined 195 Sonar and automatic flight control package.

The 'Leander' class frigates in some cases will have an enhanced anti-submarine armament with the fitting of IKARA in place of their twin 4.5in gun turret. But air defence in the 'Leander' class is poor in comparison with that in contemporary Russian ships while Russian short-range surface-to-surface missile systems probably outrange the 4.5in. The AS.12 missile in these ships' 'Wasp' (to be replaced by 'Lynx') helicopters had a marginally greater range than Soviet surface-to-air missiles in service some three years ago. But the margin is a narrow one.

With the advent of all-gas turbine propulsion in the Type 42 and Type 21 ships there should be considerable improvements in speed —the 'Leander' class have been outrun by many Soviet ships—and gas turbines should confer greater ease of maintenance. The seakeeping qualities of the 'Leander' class are excellent and endurance with a modern force of Royal Fleet Auxiliary oilers is less the problem than once it was.

The Royal Fleet Auxiliary looks on a fair course to maintain a modern fleet of oilers and store ships, incidentally, and has been the recipient of some of Lord Carrington's £70 million cornucopia announced last autumn to help unemployment on Clydeside and elsewhere.*

Returning to the Type 42s and 21s, the former have a rather better surface-to-surface missile capability than the 'County' class, being equipped with SEA DART. But, again, this is basically a surface-to-air missile system. The type 21s' main advantage over the 'Leander' class is their improved electronic 'package' with the CAAIS, and the new Vickers-developed single 4.5in gun.

Of the remaining frigates only the 'Tribal' class are likely to be in service by the end of the decade. These also lack speed and have

* See A. J. Watts article on replenishment in this volume.

an armament more suited for the East of Suez role for which they were originally designed.

The amphibious forces look like remaining unchanged through the decade though *Intrepid* will probably replace the Dartmouth Training Squadron frigates in order to release some frigates for general service. *Hermes* is, of course, replacing *Bulwark* in 1974 while *Albion* may be refurbished. *Hermes* is losing her 984 Comprehensive Display System radar on the grounds that it is not needed in the Commando ship role—in view of its value for air defence purposes this would seem a retrograde step. She is also losing her arrestor wires and catapults which rules out any question of her eventually having some form of modified 'Harrier' fitted with an arrestor hook. Such an addition to the 'Harrier' configuration would help offset the heavy fuel consumption needed for vertical landings while catapult launching would make even greater reductions in fuel consumed. But the 'Harrier' as a naval weapon will be examined more closely later.

The mine countermeasures (MCM) force will be partially replaced by GRP vessels for which *Wilton* now fitting out at Vosper-Thornycroft's Southampton yard will be the trials ship—although she will be smaller than the new design envisaged. With these ships costing around £1.5 million each, many of the forty or so coastal minesweepers and hunters now in service, but performing ancillary duties outside the MCM field, and the few remaining inshore minesweepers are to be replaced by a naval version of the RAF's long-range rescue vessels *Seal*, *Sea Otter* and *Seagull*. It is to be hoped the naval version will prove less wet in heavy weather!

For some time two new support ships similar to the Australian Navy's *Stalwart* have been under consideration. But in view of the East of Suez rundown plus the likely retention of *Triumph* and *Berry Head* in reserve for some years to come, it seems unlikely orders for these ships will be placed in the comparatively near future.

To sum up, then, the Navy of the 'seventies has good anti-submarine systems; anti-air-

craft systems effective for limited point defence at comparatively short range in view of the performance of modern aircraft with stand-off air-to-surface missiles; poor surface-to-surface capabilities and little chance of any effective submarine-launched anti-surface ship system being in service inside the decade.

The new French EXOCET surface-to-surface missile has not been mentioned deliberately since it falls within what is still one of the hottest areas of controversy in the naval field; the provision of air support. EXOCET, after all, is to some degree supposed to replace the carrier strike aircraft.

In ordering EXOCET★ (in place of SEA MARTEL which, at the time it was proposed by Mr Healey in 1968 as a replacement for the carriers in 1972 was: 'no more than a sketch on the back of an envelope' and about ten years off becoming operational) the Conservative government described it—and the retention of the carrier *Ark Royal* beyond 1972—as 'filling the missile gap' left by Labour's policy. The yardstick of comparison seemingly taken for EXOCET was the STYX fitted in the Soviet (and her allies) fast missile boats and to this extent EXOCET has a marginally greater range.

Certainly, it is better than a 4.5in gun—but is this really what is needed? Do we not still require 'a surface-to-surface missile that is retractable, reusable, and self-reproducing' as one well-known American naval spokesman in London has described the carrier-borne aircraft? Only with a fixed-wing aircraft at sea do we still have a naval weapon which can outrange the kind of naval weaponry that might be used against our ships.

General Monk once wrote: "The nation that would rule upon the seas must always attack". If the Western navies, to which the Royal Navy still makes a large contribution, fail to maintain their rule upon the seas then the Western alliance must inevitably collapse. But to attack in order to maintain that rule it is essential to have the means of so doing.

Neither EXOCET nor SEA DART nor SEASLUG II in their surface-to-surface mode, nor four mile

★ See J. Marriott's article on missiles in this volume.

range torpedoes give our Navy even the remote ability to attack before our ships may themselves be attacked. These weapon systems are the inevitable product of a Navy which has been built up around carriers. Withdraw the carriers and one is left with Hamlet without the Prince of Denmark with a vengeance.

In deciding to phase out the carriers the last government was misled into believing that shore-based aircraft could fill the gap. This fallacy was finally exploded in December 1971 when four aged warships playing the part of a Russian missile ship squadron were able to roam the North Sea for days without being struck by shore-based aircraft. The reason was partly that the RAF had insuffi-

cient planes to support the Fleet *and* defend Britain against conventioned air attacks and partly that fog closed all but three major air stations in Britain for part of the 14-day exercise. Yet weather conditions at sea were such that aircraft could easily have been operated—had any been available.

Typically, the official reaction was to ban any discussion of the lessons learnt from the exercise which might support the view that seaborne aircraft remain vital.

Is the Navy therefore to become an enlarged coast defence force once *Ark Royal* is withdrawn in 1978? This fear, quite genuinely maintained by many in the Navy, would, were it to be realised, inevitably

An official model of the 'Through Deck Cruiser'. The numerous radars and large island superstructure indicate this could be a most costly ship were such a design adopted. The open forecastle casts doubts upon the weather conditions in which it is supposed the forward missile launcher could be used. Note the slight angle given to the flight deck.
[MoD, RN, Official

mean putting our Merchant Navy, our overseas interests, our political influence and ultimately our very survival at the mercy of the Soviet Union.

This cannot, presumably, be the intention of defence political leaders of either major Party—but their actions—or rather inaction—makes it decidedly doubtful if they have thought through the consequences of the present policy.

The alternative to the carriers being proposed today is the 'Through Deck Cruiser' (hereinafter TDC). This would appear to be a ship of between 12,000 and 18,000 tons displacement equipped with SEA DART for self-defence and able to carry perhaps eight vertical take-off and landing (VTOL) aircraft and a dozen 'Sea King' helicopters.

The cost will be in the order of £50 million (though a figure as high as £70 million has been mentioned) and we are assured that these ships—probably three in number—would be built anyway even if a fixed-wing VTOL aircraft was not available. If this were to be the case it would be difficult to envisage a more costly way of getting 36 helicopters to sea. If this becomes the sole purpose of these ships half a dozen ships like RFA *Engadine* built on mercantile lines would be rather more appropriate—and far less expensive.

But why the doubt about the 'Harrier' in a seaborne role? The answer is quite simply that at present this aircraft lacks both the range and weaponload to make it a worthwhile naval aircraft. At this point one of these complex issues arises due to successive governments' reluctance to approve any new weapon for the British forces unless it can first be shown to have a major overseas sale potential.

Unless the existing 'Harrier' is sold in large numbers overseas the government is unlikely to approve the development of the Pegasus 15 engine which will cost around £42 million. This engine fitted in the 'Harrier', or at least in some form of VTOL aircraft owing something to the 'Harrier' design, would help overcome many of the Navy's main objections to the 'Harrier' as it is today.

But since other navies such as those of the United States, Australia, Argentina, India and possibly Italy are aware of the possibility of a new VTOL development being in the offing they are naturally reluctant to buy the existing 'Harrier'. Fortunately, there may be a way out of this vicious circle.

When he visited London last autumn the American Secretary of the Navy, Mr John H. Chafee, made it clear that the new 'sea control' (formerly 'air capable') ships carrying about eight VTOL aircraft would go ahead and long-lead items for the first would be sought in the 1972 fiscal year with actual construction likely to start in 1974. He also emphasised that these ships would not carry the existing 'Harrier'.

From this it seems clear that America may develop the engine—if not the airframe—needed for an effective naval VTOL aircraft.

A 'Harrier' of No. 1 Squadron, RAF, with another on the flight deck aft of *HMS Ark Royal*.
[MoD, RN, Official

If this happens, and there is every indication it will, then presumably we could buy back the engine—or the complete aircraft—without incurring more than a fraction of the development costs. It should be remembered that the development of the steam catapult and angled deck was largely left to the Americans and, although British inventions, the Royal Navy was able to benefit from American research and experience.

The provision of some form of fixed-wing VTOL aircraft at sea should go some way toward giving the Navy the offensive potential it so clearly lacks today. Whether this is the best or even the most effective answer is open to question.

When the new Fleet carrier CVA-01 was cancelled in 1966 it was claimed by many that the Navy had priced itself out of the market in demanding that the new ship should have the latest equipment in a variety of fields. Though in fact the decision was as much a political as an economic one, since an alternative design costing about half CVA-01's estimated price was rejected out of hand by Mr Healey, there is a strong case for reconsidering a fixed-wing aircraft carrier design. Since 1966 an outline configuration has become available which would permit the construction of a carrier costing about £30 million based on a large container ship hull. Such a ship could be shorn of expensive air defence missile systems; command communication facilities; data processing systems; large radar arrays and ECM since all systems are available in other ships which, as noted earlier, have for the most part been *designed* to support carriers.

The kind of design envisaged would carry about twenty aircraft. The type of aircraft would be more problematical but the Anglo-French 'Jaguar' springs to mind. This is flying from the comparatively small French carriers *Foch* and *Clemenceau*. It is perhaps significant that, despite the RAF's shortage of aircraft, some notably partisan RAF protagonists in the press have suddenly begun underlining the 'Jaguar's' cost. These same gentlemen have also decried the decision to retain some 'Phantoms' and 'Buccaneers' for *Ark Royal* on the grounds that they could be better employed by the RAF—something upon which last December's maritime air defence exercise casts considerable doubts. In view of the mobility conferred upon naval aircraft by their parent carrier the cost of providing them would be less than in trying to achieve the same object with shore-based aircraft which would be needed in considerably greater numbers.

Possibly the 'Jaguar' might not be *the* answer but at present there would seem to be no other, except conceivably the Anglo-German-Italian 'Multi-Role Combat Aircraft'. It has, incidentally, been calculated that without modernisation the carrier *Centaur*, now on the scrapping list, could have operated forty 'Jaguars'. *Eagle*, also now for scrap, could probably handle as many as sixty but there is an even stronger argument for her retention; namely that at a cost of £5 million she could have been brought up to *Ark Royal's* standard to operate 'Phantoms'. This money could have come from Lord Carrington's recent £70 million handout for an accelerated construction programme—but then *Eagle* would have been refitted in a Royal Dockyard and dockyard labour forces are being run-down so they hardly qualify for unemployment relief. Without *Eagle* there will be long gaps when the Navy is bereft of any true offensive capability while *Ark Royal* refits.

Perhaps those in the Navy who believe the TDC is not the most cost effective way of giving the Fleet an offensive capability in the 1980s may be aiming too high in hoping for a partial reversal of the 1966 decision on carriers. Maybe an improved 'Harrier' will provide an adequate answer. But one thing alone is quite clear: unless the Navy is to have some form of carrying out an effective attack against hostile ships at a range and in circumstances it can largely dictate anywhere on the oceans then the maintenance of any, albeit limited, British seapower is at an end. It is as bluntly simple as that.

A Maritime VTOL Aircraft?

ANTHONY J. WATTS

In May 1971 a revolutionary aircraft underwent trials on board the aircraft carrier *Ark Royal*. The plane was the Vertical Take-Off and Landing (VTOL) 'Harrier'. Commencing on May 4th, 1971, two 'Harriers' of No 1 Squadron RAF spent ten days, averaging six sorties a day, carrying out practise landings in the Moray Firth. The main purpose of the trials was to evaluate the 'Harrier' under operational conditions in a maritime role.

The trials, which included the dropping of a 1000 lb practise bomb as part of the weapon trials, clearly showed the value of the VTOL aircraft as a means of providing protection against an over-the-horizon missile threat or against shadowing enemy forces. Although the basic trials were a success, they did show that the 'Harrier' as built at present lacks adequate range and combat payload. These problems should, however, be overcome when later production models of the 'Harrier' are fitted with the more powerful Rolls Royce Pegasus 15 engines. Further trials on board the helicopter cruiser *Blake* and the Italian *Andrea Doria* have shown that although the VTOL aircraft can be operated from hybrid carriers, a minimum landing area of 75ft long by 50ft wide is required, and that to avoid loss of power, which could reach dangerous proportions due to the jets sucking in salt water, this platform must be at least 25ft above sea level.

These later trials have shown an added bonus of the VTOL aircraft in the possible role of ground support in amphibious operations, *provided* the above conditions are met.

In addition, although originally not specifically designed for operating VTOL aircraft, the new Through-Deck Cruiser will certainly be given formidable teeth *if* it is provided with a number of VTOL planes.

'Harrier' XV795 of No. 1 Squadron, RAF, about to land on the aircraft carrier *Ark Royal* during trials undertaken in the Moray Firth. Notice the downward facing exhausts of the vertical jets.

[MoD, RN, Official

'Harrier' XV749 undergoing sea trials with the *Ark Royal* in May 1971. During the trials 57 sorties were flown from the carrier, including 21 which tested the weapons capability of the aircraft. In the photograph a 'Sea King' helicopter acts as plane guard.

[MoD, RN, Official

'Harrier' XV281 undergoing trials on board the carrier *Eagle.*

A 'Harrier' of No. 1 Squadron RAF on the flight deck of the *Ark Royal.* There are three fuselage attachment points and four underwing attachment points for stores of up to 8,000 lbs. The aircraft in the picture is fitted with two pods and a bomb under the fuselage for weapons trials.

[MoD, RN, Official

Ship-borne Air Support—The Hybrid Cruiser/Carrier

CAPTAIN D. MACINTYRE DSO

During World War II and the fifteen years following its conclusion, aircraft carriers, descended from the prototype HMS *Argus* of 1918, advanced quickly and continuously in size and technical complexity. The cost of their construction also rocketted from a typical £16 million approximately for HMS *Eagle*, laid down in 1942, to the £88½ million for the USS *Constellation* laid down in 1960 and £140 million for the nuclear-powered USS *Enterprise*.

By that time it was becoming clear that for all but the most wealthy powers—and perhaps even for them—carriers capable of operating contemporary fighting planes absorbed so much of the money available for naval strength that they put the provision of a balanced fleet beyond their means. At the same time the prodigious rise in the offensive capability of the submarine with the application of nuclear power and its equipment with cruise missiles vastly increased the problem of self-defence of such dense and costly concentrations of naval power.

During the 1960's, therefore, after a long-drawn and agonised re-appraisal, the decision to build no more fixed-wing aircraft-carriers was taken by the British government. Similar conclusions were reached by the other navies (other than the American Navy) which had acquired a carrier arm and for them all a period of 'phasing-out' set in, with the conversion of the smaller carriers to anti-submarine capabilities.

* See the article by J. D. Brown in this volume.

For these navies, and for those which had never included fixed-wing carriers, interest now naturally concentrated on Vertical Take-off and Landing (VTOL). In the absence of any fixed-wing VTOL aircraft with adequate performance for such air support as fighter defence, air strike capability and air-borne radar, reliance would have to be put on shore-based aircraft. Development of rotary-wing (helicopter) aircraft in the anti-submarine role, however, had already progressed to the stage where they could detect and attack submarines,* and a helicopter was becoming a standard feature of every escort vessel. Development was now directed to the concept of ships primarily adapted to the operation of helicopters.

Helicopters had already become essential units for any force designed to take part in amphibious intervention operations, where they would be used for landing troops and equipment. The idea of landing assault troops in helicopters carried in the same ships as the troops had first been experimented with during the Korean War by the Americans, using a World War II escort carrier. A practical demonstration by the British was given during the Anglo-French intervention in Egypt at the time of the Suez crisis in 1956. There No 45 RM Commando and equipment—415 men and 23 tons of stores—were put ashore by helicopters from the light fleet carriers *Theseus* and *Ocean* in ninety minutes.

The success of this operation led to the decision to convert the light fleet carriers *Bulwark* and *Albion* into the first of a new class of ships known as Commando Carriers between 1959 and 1962, each of which could accommodate one RM Commando and operate twenty helicopters and four landing craft. The American Navy took up the idea at about the same time and in April 1959 laid down the *Iwo Jima*, the first of a class of seven amphibious assault ships (LPH) to be built over the next nine years. These ships can carry a Marine battalion landing team with its guns, vehicles and equipment and a reinforced squadron of 28–32 transport helicopters. Though specifically designed and constructed

Following the Suez operations of 1956 when two light fleet carriers off-loaded No. 45 RM Commando helicopter plans were drawn up to convert the light carriers *Bulwark* and *Albion*. The *Bulwark* is shown refuelling from the RFA *Tidepool*.

[MoD, RN, Official

The *Iwo Jima* is one of seven amphibious assault ships built for the American Navy and capable of carrying a Marine battalion landing team with all its weapons and equipment. Unlike the British Commando ships, these vessels carry no landing craft.

[Official USN

The *Denver* is one of the new LPDs of the 'Austin' class. These vessels have no built-in capability for carrying helicopters, but can operate up to six such aircraft when carrying out amphibious operations. *[Lockheed SB & Construction Co.*

for the purpose, they are basically similar to small fixed-wing carriers.

In June 1960 the American Navy broke new ground with the laying-down of the *Raleigh*, the first of three Amphibious Transports, Dock (LPD) with a docking well aft for landing craft and capable of carrying some 900 troops and a number of vehicles. Over the docking well is a flight deck from which six 'Sea King' helicopters can be operated.

The first of a larger class of LPD's, the USS *Austin* of 16,900 tons displacement at full load, was laid down in February 1963 and was followed by eleven more of the same type over the next three years. None of these ships has a built-in hanger for helicopters, or aircraft maintenance facilities, but operate six helicopters sent to them from accompanying LPH's or the (newer) LHA's mentioned below. They can also carry various combinations of landing craft—eg twenty amphibious tracked vehicles (LVT) or one tank landing craft (LCU) and six landing craft (LCM).

Meanwhile the British need for replacements for the Royal Navy's ageing and dwindling force of war-built landing ships and craft, had led to the laying-down in December 1961 of HMS *Fearless*, the first British LPD or Assault Ship. This ship and her sister, *Intrepid*, of 11,060 tons displacement, besides being able to carry fifteen tanks, a score of vehicles and eight landing craft and a RM Commando or infantry battalion, have, over the well-deck aft from which the landing craft are floated out, a flight deck with facilities for operating five helicopters. They have also some of the important features of the cruiser such as spacious operations rooms and sophisticated communications equipment.

Such ships, which have the single function of amphibious warfare, cannot really be classed amongst the hybrid ships we are mainly concerned with. Nor can such ships as the Escort Cruisers laid down in 1958 for the Italian Navy—*Andrea Doria* and *Caio Duilio*. Though they constitute steps in the progress towards the hybrid ships, they are, in fact, simply large versions of the escort vessel, capable of operating—but not, in the absence of any hangar, of maintaining—four Anti-Submarine Warfare (ASW) helicopters instead of only one.

They are not intended to supply air power to a naval force at sea in place of the fixed-wing carriers; and, indeed, they were laid down well before the British decision to phase out the Royal Navy's carrier force. The first post-war developments towards finding a partial substitute for the fixed-wing carrier were made by navies which had, in fact either a very limited carrier force or never had any—the French, Italian and the Russian. Except for the fact that the ships were designed for operation of VTOL aircraft types, they were a hark-back to the early cruiser/carrier of 1918, HMS *Vindictive* which, with a flying-off deck forward of the bridge and a landing-on deck and hangar abaft her after funnel, still

retained a proportion of her cruiser armament of 7.5in guns and torpedo tubes. Other early examples of hybrid ships were the Japanese battleships *Ise* and *Hyuga* which, during the Second World War, similarly sacrificed their two after turrets to accommodate a hangar and flight-deck. In their case, however, they were intended to operate floatplane dive-bombers which were catapulted off and re-embarked by crane after alighting alongside.

The first post-war hybrid ships have been cruisers designed or converted for the operation of helicopters, the French Navy showing the way with the *Jeanne d'Arc*, a cruiser-helicopter carrier of 10,000 tons standard displacement laid down in 1960, which incorporates a flight-deck and hangar from her superstructure aft with a lift for transfer of aircraft between the two. She mounts an armament of four 100mm automatic guns as well as a twin launcher for MASURCA surface-to-air missiles situated forward of the bridge. The

The *Portland* landing ship dock of the 'Anchorage' class, like most new amphibious warfare vessels in the American navy, is equipped to operate helicopters, but not to carry or maintain them.

[*General Dynamics*

Jeanne d'Arc's peacetime function is as a training ship in which capacity she carries only four helicopters; in war-time she would carry eight and could fulfil the role of anti-submarine helicopter carrier or Commando Carrier.

It was perhaps the example of the *Jeanne d'Arc* which led to a simultaneous, similar conception by the British, Italian and Russian navies around 1965. The British took advantage of their possession of three 9,500 ton cruisers laid down in 1941 and 1942, but not completed until 1959–61, for whose primarily gun armament no top priority purpose seemed to exist in a missile age; these they decided to convert to command helicopter cruisers, though only two—the *Blake* and the *Tiger*—were in the event to be so treated.

Forward of the mainmast these ships have retained their cruiser characteristics, retaining one twin turret housing 6-inch fully auto-matic dual purpose guns and one twin 3in turret similarly automatic, both types developing a very high rate of fire. Their missile armament comprises two quadruple SEACAT launchers. In place of the superstructure aft a box-shaped hangar and workshop opens on to a flight deck erected over the quarter-deck and extending to the stern. Four 'Sea King' anti-submarine helicopters can be operated and maintained.

The inspiration for the conversion of these cruisers came clearly from the looming dissolution of the Royal Navy's carrier force; though their very limited air capability does little to fill the gap left by this loss, they do share one of the carrier's important characteristics, the ability to provide a suitable vehicle from which the complex business of command of a modern naval force can be exercised.

The Italian ship of similar type is the 7,500 ton *Vittorio Veneto*, laid down in 1965 which,

The British *Intrepid* is similar to the American vessels of the 'Austin' class. Like the American vessels, their British counterparts are fitted with a flight deck from which helicopters can be operated, but are not themselves fitted with hangars or maintenance facilities.   *[MoD RN, Official*

from the after 'MACK' (combined mast and smoke-stack) forward is a guided missile cruiser with surface-to-air TERRIER missiles, surface-to-surface NETTUNO missiles, eight 3in AA guns and six anti-submarine torpedo tubes. Abaft the after MACK is a helicopter flight deck connected by two lifts with a hangar beneath it, whence nine ASW helicopters can be operated.

Laid down at about the same time was the *Moskva* for the Russian Navy, followed by her sister ship *Leningrad*, which were commissioned in 1967 and 1968 respectively. Some 20,000 tons displacement at full load, these ships, also, are powerful guided-missile cruisers with two surface-to-air systems of twin launchers and one twin launcher for either surface-to-surface or ASW missiles, and four 57mm automatic AA guns, while aft they are equipped to operate a score of ASW helicopters from a flight deck connected by

two lifts with the hangar immediately below.

The size of these ships and their lavish electronic equipment would suggest that they are also designed to function as force flagships or, alternatively, could operate in an amphibious role.

This completes the catalogue of existing cruiser-carriers of the world's navies. One function of the aircraft carrier for which, to some extent, they provide a substitute, is that of command and control of a naval force, including both the surface units and the aircraft deployed in support. But how far, it must be asked, do any of them go towards providing substitutes for ship-borne air support of the aircraft carrier, namely, long-range strategic strike, reconnaissance, fighter-defence, ship strike, Air-borne Early Warning (AEW) and ASW? So long as they are equipped with rotary-wing aircraft, the answer must be only ASW and possibly AEW. Though

The Italian *Andrea Doria* is an escort cruiser capable of operating four ASW helicopters.

[Italian Navy, Official

Although nominally a training ship carrying four helicopters, the French *Jeanne d'Arc* can quickly be adapted to operate as a commando carrier or ASW vessel carrying about 10 helicopters.

[French Navy, Official

helicopters of the 'Sea King' size can be equipped as air-to-surface missile launchers, they could obviously not be pitted against ships with a modern missile and gun AA system. The currently accepted dogma on maritime air operations in the absence of fixed-wing carriers is for all air support other than ASW to be provided by shore-based aircraft. Except for long-range strategic strike, which should never have been a carrier task, and AEW, a large body of naval opinion does not accept the validity of that concept.

Short-range ship strike is a vitally necessary capability for the defence of a naval force, in that it is the only really effective weapon against the small, cheap patrol craft supplied by Russia to her allies, satellites and dependants, equipped with surface-to-surface missiles. Even if a surface-to-surface missile were available to the Royal Navy (which, as a result of previous dependence upon carrier-borne aircraft, it is not), the advantage would still lie with these small craft with their insignificant radar silhouette.* They would be very vulnerable on the other hand to a rocket-firing fighter aircraft.

Both for fighter defence against air attack and for short range strike, speed of reaction to any given threat is of the essence. With aircraft for each of these to be provided from shore-bases, this would require them to be constantly air-borne over the naval force and under control of the naval force commander. This could no doubt be achieved at moderate ranges from the aircrafts' base; it is envisaged, however, for ranges up to 500 nautical miles, a situation which must be of doubtful feasibility to say the least, calling for airborne refuelling on every sortie and a great deal of wasteful flying time. It is to be hoped that the situation may yet be restored by the introduction of the comparatively cheap carrier operating V/STOL aircraft.

The latter, with a performance and pay load

* See J. Marriott's article on missiles.

46

The command helicopter cruiser *Blake* is equipped to maintain and operate four anti-submarine helicopters. The after superstructure was replaced by a hangar and a raised flight deck built out over the stern. *[A. J. Watts*

The Italian *Vittorio Veneto* is similar in configuration to the British converted 'Tiger' class cruisers. Being designed from the outset for operating helicopters, however, she can carry a total of nine such aircraft. *[Italian Navy, Official*

The Russian cruiser helicopter carrier *Moskva* is again similar to the Italian and British vessels, being equipped with a hangar and flight deck aft. These vessels are designed particularly with anti-sub-marine operations in mind, being capable of carrying and operating up to 20 ASW helicopters as well as being armed with anti-submarine torpedoes, missiles and variable depth sonar. *[MoD, RN, Official*

good enough to provide fighter-defence, and alternatively a short-range strike capability, has not yet emerged. The seed from which it may grow, the 'Hawker Harrier', is in service, however, with the Royal Air Force and the United States Marines; and, on the assumption that such a development will occur, a suitable ship is under design for the Royal Navy. No doubt to avoid any resurgence of the bitter controversy that preceded the abolition of the carrier, it is currently referred to as a 'Through-Deck Cruiser'; but with its superstructure and funnels rising from the starboard edge of an unobstructed flight deck extending from the stern almost the full length of the ship, this 15 to 20,000-ton project with its facilities for a limited take-off and landing run will seem to many a small fixed-wing carrier.* Nevertheless the planned armament of a quadruple surface-to-surface missile launcher and two twin SEA DART missiles will give it the fire power of a cruiser, while there should be ample space for force command capabilities.

* See picture page 35.

One matter in doubt, however, is how 'comparatively cheap' is this ship likely to be? And are the limited funds available to the Royal Navy to be concentrated on provision of one or two high performance hybrid ships or on a larger number of cheaper ones? According to Jane's Fighting Ships, the projected ship is to be propelled by gas turbine engines at 30+ knots. This must surely entail a hull design calling for high-grade materials and ship-construction techniques as well as a costly engineering plant the whole of which must add up to expensive production and maintenance?

Comparable ships are the United States LPH's of the *Iwo Jima* class and the LDA's still under construction. These are both classified as Amphibious Assault Ships; but both types could be adapted to operate V/STOL fixed-wing aircraft. Their speed at about twenty knots (sustained) is unambitious, but need not be a bar to their employment in certain types of operation as suppliers of air support in whatever roles V/STOL aircraft become capable of undertaking. In the case

An artist's impression of the new American LHA amphibious warfare vessel that is equipped with a full length flight deck, a docking well, and a large garage for the storage of troop vehicles. *[Official USN*

of the *Iwo Jima*, this characteristic permitted the hull to be of simple design and construction similar to that of escort carriers of World War II, while the motive power is the well-tried geared turbine. The cost, therefore, was kept down to approximately £14.3 million in 1961, equivalent to-day (1972) to say £20 million—still very good value for the money. Furthermore, it avoids putting at risk in one package too much operational potential as well as money and thus becomes comparatively 'expendable'.

When we come to consider what is known of the new LHA's being built for the United States Navy, we find a far more versatile as well as a larger and more complicated design. More than 39,000 tons (full load), they not only have a full-length flight deck and a hangar suitable for the operation and maintenance of a large number of helicopters and/or V/STOL fixed-wing aircraft, but also a landing craft docking well, a large garage for trucks and armoured vehicles and will be able to accommodate a reinforced battalion of 63 officers and 622 men. They will undoubtedly have command and control facilities.

Provision of such a range of capabilities is proving expensive, cost estimates for LHA2 and 3 being £65 million each, a sum which puts them far out of the 'expendable' class, even for the American Navy, and would be far beyond the resources of smaller navies. Perhaps the test of the validity of such an expensive unit is the extent to which it is capable of providing its own defence. The low (20+) knot speed of the LHA's and the unhandiness that may go with it in such a large ship are handicaps when under threat by submarines; and though a proportion of the helicopters borne will no doubt be equipped for ASW, this will be at the expense of the ship's Amphibious Warfare efficiency and will in any case not obviate the necessity for surface escorts. Capability to defend themselves against air- or ship- or submarine-borne missile attack will depend upon any improvements that may be made to the design of V/STOL aircraft in the future.

The American Navy, however, continuing to provide its own main air support from the decks of aircraft carriers, has little incentive to look upon its LHA's as anything other

49

HMS Blake.

than Amphibious Assault Ships which will be able to rely upon the sheltering wing of the fleet for defence.

The British Royal Navy, on the other hand, must look upon any such ship as the hard core around which a Task Group would be gathered. With the number of surface escorts likely to be available there will be frequent occasions when this 'capital ship' will be left with, at best, one or two on her screen. Faced with the threat from nuclear submarines with high submerged speed and good manoeuvrability, only high speed and frequent radical manoeuvres on her own part will then offer any hope of immunity.

So the '30+' maximum speed is essential; and it is this, combined with the powerful missile armament projected that must make the 'through-deck cruiser' unique as the first of a new generation of fixed-wing carriers, cheaper (though surely far from 'cheap') and adapted for operation of less sophisticated fighting aircraft than the fleet carriers of the 60's, yet fulfilling their main functions. With its advent, the Royal Navy may again become a self-dependent force for all purposes except ocean air patrol and surveillance.

Everything will depend, however, on the effort given to development of V/STOL in the next few years. Like so many British revolutionary concepts, however, the high cost of research and development is delivering it into United States hands; the Royal Navy is thus liable once again to find itself depending on American good-will to equip its Fleet Air Arm.

Nevertheless, the ships are on the drawing-board; it can hardly be imagined that suitable aircraft for them will not be forthcoming. It could be, therefore, that the 'hybrid cruiser' really represents the rationalisation of the aircraft carrier concept, calling a halt to the upward spiral of size, sophistication and cost in favour of a vessel designed to provide only the ship-borne air support required by naval forces which have no strategic strike role. For the time being, it is true, the role officially visualised for such a ship is to take the place of the vanished carrier or cruiser as a command and control ship and to operate ASW helicopters such as the 'Sea King' at present in service. An interesting era of experimentation may nevertheless be ahead.

The 'Tiger' Class

P. A. VICARY

World War II was almost over when three new cruisers were launched for the Royal Navy. The first to enter the water was named the *Defence*, launched from Scotts Shipbuilding Co. Clyde on September 2nd, 1944. The second ship, the *Tiger* (ex-*Bellerophon*), was launched from John Brown's Yard, Clydebank, on October 25th, 1945. The *Blake* (ex-*Tiger*, ex-*Blake*) was the last to be launched from Fairfields on the Clyde on December 20th, 1945.

Work on all three cruisers was suspended from July 1946, and the ships were towed away to be laid up for about eight years. The *Defence* went to the Gareloch, the *Tiger* to Dalmuir, and the *Blake* to Greenock.

In 1957 the *Defence* was towed from the Gareloch to Swan Hunters Yard on the Tyne, and was renamed HMS *Lion* on October 8th, 1957, the ship being completed on July 20th, 1960.

The *Tiger* was eventually completed on March 18th, 1959, and the *Blake* on March 8th, 1961, and originally cost in the region of £14 million.

Early in 1965, HMS *Blake* was taken in hand for conversion to a Helicopter Support Ship at Portsmouth, a job which took four years to complete, and cost another £5 million, before she re-commissioned on April 23rd, 1969. The reconstruction involved the suppression of her after 6in turret and the two 3in turrets amidships. A raised flight deck and hangar to accommodate four helicopters was erected aft, making her look a little ungainly, and causing her to be nicknamed the 'Push-me, Pull-you'.

The *Tiger* has undergone a similar conversion at Devonport and commissioned for sea in May 1972. The *Lion* whose proposed conversion was deferred is now awaiting the decision as to whether or not she will be scrapped.

TABLE. (As completed)

DISPLACEMENT: 9550 (standard/11700 (full load) tons.
DIMENSIONS: 555½ (oa) × 64 × 21ft.
SPEED: 31½ knots
ARMAMENT: Four 6in (2 × 2), six 3in (3 × 2) guns.

SHIP	LAID DOWN	LAUNCHED	COMPLETED
Tiger	1.10.41	25.10.45	18.3.59
Lion	24.6.42	2.9.44	20.7.60
Blake	17.8.42	21.12.45	8.3.61

(As converted)

DISPLACEMENT: 9500 (standard)/12080 (full load) tons.
DIMENSIONS: 566½ (oa) × 64 × 23ft.
SPEED: 31½ knots (maximum)
ARMAMENT: Two 6in (1 × 2), two 3in (1 × 2) guns; eight SEACAT (2 × 4) guided missile launchers; four Wessex helicopters.

SHIP	CONVERSION COMMENCED	CONVERSION COMPLETED
Tiger	1968	25.5.72
Lion	Conversion cancelled	
Blake	early 1965	23.4.69

HMS Defence (later renamed *Lion*) lying partially completed in the Gareloch.

[P. A. Vicary

HMS *Blake* fitting out at Fairfields yard on the Clyde July 8, 1960. Notice completely redesigned bridge and lattice masts in place of tripods to have been fitted as originally designed. New 6-inch and 3-inch guns are fitted in place of designed original armament.

[P. A. Vicary

HMS *Tiger* entering Portsmouth harbour on March 25, 1959 just after commissioning. The 6-inch gun plainly visible has a rate of fire of 20 rounds per minute.

[P. A. Vicary

HMS *Tiger* at Greenock June 30, 1966. Notice new fire control equipment for the after 6-inch and broadside 3-inch guns.   *[P. A. Vicary*

HMS *Blake* after conversion to command helicopter cruiser. From the mainmast to the stern has been rebuilt with a large hangar in place of the original after superstructure, and a raised flight deck built over the stern. The Type 960 long range air warning radar has been replaced by the more up to date Type 965 with its associated bedstead aerial.   *[P. A. Vicary*

The *Blake* and *Tiger* have had their midships 3-inch replaced by a quadruple 'Seacat' launcher. The fire control system for the 3-inch has been retained and incorporates the GWS 22 fire control system in which the binocular sight of the aimer is linked to a lock and follow tracking radar.

[A. J. Watts

Ship Missiles—The Surface-to-Surface Problem

JOHN MARRIOTT

For centuries the standard method of engagement between surface ships has been by means of the gun. In the old days the range was short, the guns were pointed in the general direction of the enemy and heavy solid shot was fired. With the development of explosives the range got longer and longer until it attained upwards of 30,000 yards. At this range there was an appreciable time of flight of the shell, so complicated computing devices were developed in order to aim off the guns to allow for the enemy's movement during the shell's flight. Such devices, of course, relied absolutely on the enemy maintaining the course and speed he was on at the moment of firing. If he made a violent alteration of course seconds after firing, the shell might miss. To a certain extent this contingency was allowed for by firing a salvo of shells which were spread over a small area, but, apart from being expensive, it left a great deal to chance.

When the development of missiles started the concentration of effort was on engaging

A 'Sea Dart' launch. 'Sea Dart' is the Royal Navy's newest missile. It is primarily a ship-to-air weapon, but has a ship-to-ship capability.

[Hawker Siddeley Dynamics

The First Sea Lord, Admiral Sir Michael Pollock,
visiting the 'Sea Dart' trials site at Woomera, Australia.

[MoD, RN, Official

aircraft. Because of their very high speed it was obviously essential that some form of guidance of the missile in flight would be necessary to ensure a hit and various methods were developed. It was, however, some time before it was realised that similar methods could be applied to engaging surface craft. In fact it was the sinking of the Israeli destroyer *Eilath* on October 21st (Trafalgar Day), 1967, by a Russian made STYX missile fired from an Egyptian 'Osa' class patrol boat that really woke the Western world up and made them realise that here was a weapon which so far they had sorely neglected.

Guidance

To discuss ship-to-ship missiles it is first necessary to outline the various methods of guidance available, since these have a large effect on the design of the missile.

There are seven methods of ship missile guidance: Beam Riding, Semi-Active Homing, Active Homing, Infra-Red Homing, Anti-Radar Homing, Radio Command and Inertial Navigation.

'Exocet' being fired from the French trials ship *La Combattante*. 'Exocet' has been ordered by the British and a number of other navies.

In the Beam Riding system the ship illuminates the target with her radar and fires the missile along the radar beam. Sensors in the missile detect the radar beam and, when the missile tries to move out of it, corrects it by delicate movements of the ailerons and rudder.

Semi-Active Homing means that the target is illuminated by the ship's radar as before, but the missile is fitted with a radar receiver which detects the waves reflected from the target by virtue of the ship's radar beam falling on it. The missile uses these reflected waves to guide itself onto the target.

Active Homing is similar except that the missile has its own radar and instead of the ship illuminating the target the missile does so itself. The advantages of this method is that it is not necessary for the ship's radar to illuminate the target during the whole of the missile's flight, and provided the missile's own radar can search for the target and lock onto it—a hit should result. The disadvantage is that it is expensive.

Infra-Red Homing also does not need the firing ship's radar. Here the missile has a

[Aerospatiale

sensitive IR (Infra-Red) receiver which scans the sea and, when it detects an object emitting infra-red waves, locks onto it and guides the missile on. IR waves are emitted by any hot object; since a ship or aircraft is naturally hotter than its surroundings it is likely to emit considerable IR radiation.

Anti-Radar Homing implies that the missile homes onto the radar transmissions of the target. This can be very useful against a ship, as any ship, faced with a possible missile attack, would be likely to use her radar in order to get early warning of the missile's approach. Provided the enemy's frequencies are known it is not difficult to fit the missile with a receiver which will home the missile onto the enemy's transmissions.

Radio Command means that the missile is guided by commands from the ship transmitted by radio by an operator. This involves the operator being able to 'see' both the missile and the target, either by eye, television or radar. The normal method is for the operator to have a small joystick which he moves in the direction he wants the missile to go; movements of this stick automatically transmit radio commands to the missile. The system depends very much on the skill of the operator.

Inertial Navigation is a method of guiding the missile in flight from one point to another by an inertial navigation system fitted in the missile. The firing ship has to set on the missile's navigational system the coordinates of the position of the firing ship and the estimated position of the enemy at the end of the missile's run. The missile's navigational system will then take it to this position, but the enemy may alter course during flight, thus combined with this system there must be some form of homing, either active radar or infra-red, or possibly anti-radar.

Each type of guidance has its advantages and disadvantages, but with modern methods of jamming it may not always be possible to illuminate the target with radar all the time, hence active-radar homing, or infra-red homing, combined with inertial navigation are now coming to the fore.

Active radar homing can, however, also be jammed, and there is always the chance that the missile will select the wrong ship on which to home. Similarly an infra-red homer will chose the target emitting the strongest IR rays and this may not necessarily be the ship it is desired to hit. IR can also be deceived by dropping (or towing) some sort of a flare which will emit stronger IR rays than the ship herself.

Thus it is not really possible to launch a missile hundreds of miles away and expect it to hit the right target relying solely on its built-in self-homer. Up to the present, therefore, really long range, or cruise missiles as they are called, have had to have some form of mid-course guidance and in fact this is what the Russians do with their cruise missiles (see below).

Missile Philosophy
As a direct result of the *Eilath* sinking, France, Italy, Norway and Israel started developing their own ship-to-ship missiles, but Britain and America argued that the best way of attacking a surface vessel was from the air.

America, of course, is well endowed with carrier borne strike aircraft, but the British, even in 1967, knew that the writing was on the wall for their fixed wing Fleet Air Arm, and it seems extraordinary that the British naval planners were unable to realise that the ship-to-ship missile would become the main armament of all navies before very long, and failed to put in train the necessary research work to enable Britain to manufacture her own.

Britain was supplying all ships of frigate size and above with helicopters, and the thinking at the time was that the best way to deal with the missile firing ship was to arm the helicopters with an air-to-ship missile. The only missile available was the French wire guided AS12 with a maximum range of five miles and the naval staff thought this was sufficient range against the patrol boat. They happily ignored the fact that against anything larger the helicopter stood little chance of

An 'Otomat' missile about to undergo wind tunnel tests. The first 'Otomat' is due to be fitted in an Italian ship in July 1973.

[Matra

approaching to within five miles without being shot down.

Sometime in 1970 the penny dropped, and the naval staff started looking around for a ship-to-ship missile which they specified would have to be in operational service by the mid '70s, when Britain's carriers would finally be faded out.

The helicopter was not, however, entirely forgotten, although it was realised that a much longer range missile was required. Britain and France, working together, therefore called for proposals for such a weapon which was required to be self homing. Its range was to be sufficient for the helicopter to stay outside the range of the target ship's weapons, and it had to be light enough to be carried by ship borne helicopters. Three firms

are doing studies: the British Aircraft Corporation, Hawker Siddeley's and France's Aerospatiale, and the two Governments will evaluate these and select a lead contractor. The development and production will be carried out jointly by the two countries.

Britain's Choice

At the time (mid 1970) when the naval staff finally realised that Britain would have to have ship-to-ship missiles there were only three possible missiles under development and one under study. They were: PENGUIN, a Norwegian development, the Italian SEA KILLER MK II and EXOCET being developed by Aerospatiale in France. Under study by Hawker Siddeley Dynamics was SHIP MARTEL.

SHIP MARTEL, which was to be a development of the well known air-to-ground MARTEL, had a great deal to commend it. Hawker Siddeley's, who were doing the study by themselves with no help from the Government, showed that they could use the air launched missile and fit it off the deck of the firing ship. They also proposed to develop an active radar homing head in place of the air missile's television or anti-radar head.

Whilst the whole project was attractive, the time scale quoted for the development was considered too long, for, with the best will in the world, Hawker Siddeley Dynamics could not guarantee that it would be in service by the mid '70s. Thus the only British missile was out.

PENGUIN was far more advanced and was cheap as missiles go, but it was rejected as its range of twelve nautical miles was not considered sufficient, and it did not have a very low trajectory, making it more easily detectable by the target's radar.

SEA KILLER also only had a range of twelve miles and it was not a self homer, so it too was rejected.

This left EXOCET which the French said would be operational by mid 1973. EXOCET had everything: long range, low trajectory, active radar homing and an in-service date which fitted with the British requirements. The naval staff therefore decided on it and on June 3rd, 1971, it was announced that 'agreement has been reached on the terms of a contract for procurement of the EXOCET system . . . . Decisions have therefore been taken to purchase the EXOCET ship system for wide fitting in frigates and larger ships with a sufficient number of missiles to provide them with a surface-to-surface capability well into the 1980s'.

Although the final decision was not taken until June 1971, a decision in principle to use EXOCET was taken in late 1970, but it took six months of hard bargaining with the French to ensure that British firms got some part of

A 'Sea Killer Mk II' missile undergoing flight tests. The missile is made by Sistel of Italy, but the control equipment is made by Contraves of Switzerland.

[Sistel, S.p.A.

the development and production. In fact Britain is only going to get less than a quarter of the work.

In the meantime another missile suddenly appeared on the horizon. Oto-Melara of Italy and Egins Matra of France announced that they were developing a new missile called OTOMAT. Details of this missile are given below and it will be seen that OTOMAT is very similar in size and price to EXOCET, but has a considerably longer range. Its in-service date is also mid 1973, but as the development had started later, EXOCET had already captured the imagination, not only of Britain but of other nations and many of them, including Britain, had gone too far to withdraw.

Although there were only four possibilities for Britain, there are in fact three other missiles under development or in-service. All the ship-to-ship missiles are listed in the table on page 00 and a glance at this table will show these three could not be considered. GABRIEL, the Israeli missile, was impossible on political grounds. Rb08, the Swedish missile, is much too large, too slow and has too long a range. The final one, the American HARPOON has only just started development and its in-service date is much too far away.

It is interesting to note that even America, albeit late in the day, has decided that she must have ship-to-ship missiles. Not only has she made the decision to develop her own as a long term project, but has also decided that she needs something in the meantime. With this in view she is studying both EXOCET and OTOMAT. EXOCET would appear to be winning as the Boing Company has obtained a licence from Aerospatiale to manufacture it in the States.

There are other missiles which have a dual role of anti-air and anti-ship. Britain's SEASLUG MK II and her new SEADART both have an anti-ship capability, so too does the American STANDARD missile and the shorter range SEA SPARROW, but none of these can be compared with a missile specifically designed as the main surface armament, and there is always the possibility that a ship might have to engage aircraft and ships at the same time.

So much for the possible missiles on, or coming onto the market. Now for a more detailed description of the more important ones, and since EXOCET looks like becoming the main surface armament in a number of navies, it will be described first.

Exocet

The word EXOCET means 'flying fish' and the missile is aptly named since it literally skims the tops of the waves. It is divided into six compartments. Right forward is the homing head which contains a radar developed by Electronique Marcel Dassault, known as ADAC. It is of a novel design in that it combines in it the proximity fuze. The radar not only homes the missile but it measures the range of the target and when it gets to a preset distance explodes the charge. The radar is specially designed to cope with the 'clutter' received when the radar antenna is only a few feet above the sea and it is claimed that it will deal with sea states up to 4 or 5 (ie waves between 3 and 8ft in height). It is also fitted with anti-jamming devices.

Abaft the homing head is the forward equipment compartment, then follows the warhead which is either exploded by the homing head when in the proximity of the target, or it explodes after it has penetrated the ship's armour.

. Further aft is the sustainer motor and abaft that again the booster motor. Finally there is a rear equipment bay. The two equipment bays between them contain the inertial navigation system.

The whole is 5.12m long and has a diameter of 0.34m and a wingspan of 1m. It weighs 700 Kg at launch. Propulsion is by two solid propellant motors—a booster to launch it and a sustainer to keep it in flight—and its range is stated to be 25+ nautical miles. Its speed is subsonic.

The missile comes in a container which is mounted on the launcher and indeed forms part of it. It is controlled initially by the ship's fire control system. Basically this consists of a computer into which is fed the bearing and range of the target, plus, of course, own ship's

A 'Gabriel' sea-to-sea missile in flight.

[Israel Industries Ltd.

course and speed and the true vertical. It is to be made by Sperry in the United Kingdom.

The enemy's position, course and speed is normally obtained by the ship's radar, but the missile could be fired at a target which is outside radar range, provided a reasonably accurate position of it relative to the firing ship can be obtained, perhaps by an airborne visual or radar link.

The computer works out the course for the missile to steer and this is fed into the inertial navigation system inside the missile.

On take off the missile at first rises and then is kept at a very low level by a radio altimeter. Towards the end of its trajectory its radar is switched on and searches until it finds the target. It then locks on and steers the missile to hit.

In principle EXOCET is a fine weapon and recent trials by the French have proved it to be very successful. If all continues to go well, the Royal Navy should start fitting it in 1973. Most Navy frigates and all larger ships are to be fitted and existing ships will be retro-fitted. The price is expected to be about £80,000 per round.

Apart from Britain's order, Aerospatiale state that they have provisional orders from Germany, Greece, Malaysia, Brazil, Peru, Chile and of course France.

EXOCET's range is only marginally better than that of the radar, but the French and the Italians between them are developing a missile whose range is considerably longer than a ship's radar. It is called OTOMAT.

Otomat

The missile is a joint development of Matra (France) and Oto Melara (Italy). It will have a maximum effective range of something over forty nautical miles, although the missile itself will have sufficient fuel to fly 100 miles. It is slightly smaller than EXOCET, but in other respects is very similar. It too has inertial navigation and an active radar homer; it too flies low over the water, but it rises at the end of its trajectory so that it can dive onto the target and penetrate through the more vulnerable decks.

To make up for the fact that it may have to be fired on enemy position reports from other ships or aircraft, its radar homer is so designed that it will search an arc which covers a ship crossing at up to forty knots at whatever the range, ie at short ranges it searches a wider arc than at long ranges. Thus, provided it is fired in the right general direction of the enemy ship, the homing head should find her.

It does not have any form of proximity fuze, but its warhead is of the semi armour piercing type. Its price is likely to come out at about £83,000.

OTOMAT is expected to be operational in 1973, the first one being delivered to the Italian Navy in July of that year.

Sea Killer

SEA KILLER MK II (now nearing completion) is an improved version of the short range Mk I version, already in service with the Italian Navy, and has a range of twelve nautical miles. The missile costs only £25,000 and is designed by the Italian firm of Sistel, with its control equipment developed by Contraves of Switzerland.

It has no self-homing and is in fact a beam rider, which means that it is automatically guided by the ship's radar beam. However, if the radar is jammed or put out of action, the missile can be guided visually by means of a closed circuit television system with the missile being manoeuvred by radio commands.

Like OTOMAT, SEA KILLER'S war head is semi armour piercing. The missiles are normally mounted on a quintuple rotatable launcher, although a fixed, single launcher can be provided if desired. Two radars are necessary, one for search and the other for control of the missile.

Gabriel

Slightly more expensive at £33,000 a round comes the Israeli missile GABRIEL. The Israelis have been very secretive about GABRIEL, but it has been possible to piece together a few details. It is a reasonably small missile with what the Israelis call 'automatic homing'. It is not clear whether this is active or semi-active radar homing or even infra-red.

Unlike all the other missiles it attains supersonic speed. Two configurations can be supplied, one with a range of twelve nautical miles and the other with a range of 24 miles. The warheads are identical, the only difference in the missile being the size of the propulsion unit.

Manufactured by Israel's largest armament firm—Israeli Aircraft Industries, it is mounted in the Israeli gunboats on a three missile pedestal launcher which is rotatable, or on a fixed single launcher mounted forward. The Israelis say it has been sold to a number of countries, but refuse to specify which. They also claim it can be fired from an aircraft or the shore.

Full marks must be given to this small nation, who were the first in the field of ship-to-

The Norwegian fast patrol boat *Traust* of the 'Storm' class fitted with 6 'Penguin' missiles.

[A/S Kongsberg Vapenfabrikk

ship missiles, perhaps naturally so since one of their own ships was the first casualty. Although little is known of GABRIEL it is at least at sea and working, which is more than can be said of most of NATO's missiles.

Penguin

More advanced than the others, however, is PENGUIN. Developed by Kongsberg Vapenfabrik of Norway with the help of America and Germany, PENGUIN has an inertial navigation system and an infra-red homing head which guides the missile to hit at the water line so as to inflict maximum damage. Its height above the water is controlled by a laser altimeter, but it is not a wave skimmer. Like so many other missiles its range is twelve nautical miles.

It is primarily designed for small craft and is being fitted in the Norwegian 'Snogg' class of motor torpedo boats. Later 20 'Storm' class of gunboats will be equipped and finally five 'Oslo' class frigates.

Harpoon

Finally there is the American McDonnell Douglas HARPOON. Two versions are to be produced, one for fitting in aircraft (both carrier borne and land based) and the other for fitting in ships. Like EXOCET and OTOMAT it will be guided initially by inertial navigation and will carry out final homing by active radar. No other details have been released except that it will have an 'over the horizon' range, but this is probably no more than 25 to 30 miles. Production is expected to start in 1975 and it should be in service in 1977.

Soviet Missiles

So much for the West's inventory, now let us look at what the Russians are doing. All the names used below are assigned by NATO and are not the real Russian names.

The first Soviet missile to make its appearance was the STYX. It has a comparatively slow speed and is probably fitted with an active radar homer. Its range is thought to be not more than about twelve nautical miles. It is fitted in the 'Komar' and 'Osa' patrol boats

of the Soviet Navy and probably also in similar boats supplied to Poland, Indonesia, Cuba and, of course, Egypt.

The guided missile ships proper are fitted either with STRELA or SHADDOCK. STRELA is the older of the two and is fitted in the 'Krupny' and 'Kildin' class destroyers in apparently two single launchers. STRELA's range is estimated to be about 100 miles and it presumably has inertial navigation and some form of self homing device, though mid-course guidance must also be necessary.

SHADDOCK was developed for maritime use from a ground-to-ground missile. It is thought to be between 30 and 40ft long and is fitted in the 'Kresta' and 'Kynda' class destroyers. In the 'Kresta' class there are two twin launchers, but the 'Kynda' class has two quadruple launchers, one forward and one aft.

SHADDOCK's range has been variously estimated at between 150 and 400 miles, but probably its maximum effective range is about 350 miles. In confined waters, such as the Mediterranean, though, it would probably not be fired at ranges of much more than 150 miles.

It is thought that it must be guided by inertial navigation initially and probably has some form of self-homing. However, it seems fairly certain that when it gets to the target area it must be tracked by an aircraft who takes over its guidance to ensure that it does not home onto the wrong target—a technique known as mid-course guidance.

This would seem to be a weakness as it presupposes that the aircraft has the enemy on its radar, which means that it would also be under surveillance by the enemy's radar. It is unlikely that, in the presence of aircraft carriers or guided missile anti-aircraft ships, the guiding aircraft could maintain its position for very long.

SHADDOCK, or some derivative of it with a much shorter range, is also fitted in a large number of submarines of the 'E1', 'E2', 'J' and 'W' classes. The larger submarines have six missiles and the smaller four.

A new Soviet missile has recently been seen in a new class of ship, the 'Krivak' class. It is

The Russian 'Krupny' class destroyer *Gnevny*.
Two surface-to-surface missile launchers can be
seen, one forward and one aft. The missiles are
'Strelas', one of the Russian's original missiles.

[*MoD, RN, Official*

A Russian 'Kresta I' class guided missile ship.
The surface-to-surface missiles are launched from
a position abreast the bridge, and there are twin
launchers either side. The two prominent launchers
forward and aft are for 'Goa', ship-to-air missiles.

[*MoD, RN, Official*

The effect of a 'Penguin' missile. The target was the old Norwegian destroyer *Haugesund* (ex-British *Beaufort*). 'Penguin' is in full production and has been fitted to a number of Norwegian fast patrol boats.

/A/S Kongsberg Vapenfabrikk

quite small and is fitted in a quadruple launcher forward in the ship. It is thought to be a short range ship-to-ship missile, probably no more than to the horizon. The same missile in similar launchers has also been seen in the 'Kresta II' class, which is a redesign of the older 'Kresta' guided missile ship. The new missile replaces the SHADDOCK's previously fitted in the 'Kresta' class.

The advent of a short range ship-to-ship missile in the Soviet Navy is causing no little interest in NATO naval circles, since all along they have maintained that the very long range cruise missiles were not really viable, because of the problems of mid-course guidance. That is not to say that such missiles are not of tactical value. Obviously, if it is possible to sink a ship from hundreds of miles away,

considerable tactical advantage would be obtained, but until a method of guidance has been developed which will ensure that the right ship is hit and does not depend upon something as vulnerable as an aircraft, NATO navies are sticking to horizon (or marginally over the horizon) missiles.

Guns

Whilst the accent these days is on missiles, the gun has not been entirely forgotten. A gun is still a useful weapon for cold or limited war use. One cannot fire a missile across a ship's bows to order it to stop; nor would it be economical to use a missile to shoot at, say, a pirate dhow. There is also a use for a gun in shore bombardment and as an anti-aircraft or anti-missile weapon. The NATO navies therefore have by no means forgotten the gun, and most ships will continue to be fitted with at least one.

Modern guns are very different from those used in World War II. Size has been kept down to between 3 and 5in and the tendency is to make the gun fully automatic.

The latest British gun, the Vickers Mark 8, is fully automatic, can fire 25 shells a minute and can be controlled from the operations room. It can even open fire under Ops Room control with no crew closed up at all.

The year to come should see EXOCET's and OTOMAT's trials nearly completed and it should be possible to assess more accurately their relative merits, in particular whether OTOMAT can really find its target 'over the horizon'. At the same time NATO should have gleaned further information on the new Soviet short range missile. Is it 'over the horizon'? What method of guidance does it have? Has it got a wave skimming trajectory? What is its speed? All these questions need to be answered before a true comparison between it and NATO's missiles can be made.

To a student of ship missile systems the forthcoming years should be interesting indeed

Western Ship-to-ship Missiles

Missile	Manufacturer	Weight in Kg	Range in Nautical Miles	Speed	Guidance	Price per Round
EXOCET	Aerospatiale (France)	700	25	0.9 mach	Inertial Nav. and active radar homing	£80,000
OTOMAT	Matra (France) Oto Melara (Italy)	600	40–50	Subsonic	ditto	£83,000
SEA KILLER Mk II	Contraves Sistel (Italy)	267	12	Subsonic	Beam riding or visual	£25,000
GABRIEL	Israeli Aircraft Industries	396	12 or 24	Supersonic	Active or semi-active radar homing	£33,000
PENGUIN	Kongsberg Vapenfabrik (Norway)	337	12	Subsonic	Inertial Nav. and IR homing	£35,000
RB 08	SAAB (Sweden)	1125	150	Subsonic	Inertial Nav. and active radar homing?	?
HARPOON	McDonnell Douglas (USA)	?	'Over horizon'	?	Inertial Nav. and active radar homing	?

The County Class Destroyer

ANTHONY J. WATTS

Below: CUTAWAY OF A COUNTY CLASS DESTROYER
1 Twin 4.5-inch guns
2 Surface and air warning radar
3 Long range air warning radar
4 Height finding radar
5 'Seacat' director
6 'Seacat' launcher
7 Helicopter hangar
8 'Seaslug' control radar
9 Anti-submarine helicopter
10 'Seaslug' launcher
11 Crew's dining hall
12 'Seaslug' stowage
13 Ratings messdeck
14 Machinery control room
15 Computer room
16 Operations room

Forward superstructure of *HMS London*. Forward
'B' 4.5-inch turret. Enclosed bridge surmounted by
4.5-inch director. Foremast with navigational radar
topped by surface and air warning radar with pole
mast carrying ECM sensors. Note 20mm oerlikon
abreast the foremast. *[A. J. Watts collection*

Foremast and mainmast of *HMS Norfolk*. Note
different aerial for air warning radar on foremast.
Double bedstead aerial on mainmast.
[A. J. Watts collection

Mainmast of *HMS London*. Note single aerial for Type 965 air warning radar. Type 277 height finding aerial halfway down mainmast. *[A. J. Watts collection*

Quadruple 'Seacat' launcher on *HMS London*.
[A. J. Watts collection

Type 901M beam radar control radar for 'Seaslug' missiles *[A. J. Watts collection*

'Seaslug' launcher on *HMS London*.
[A. J. Watts collection

Left: Ratings messdeck on a 'County' class destroyer. *[MoD, RN, Official*

Bottom left: One of the 'lanes' down which the 'Seaslug' missile travels from the magazine to the launcher. The missiles are moved by hydraulic handling gear and a plan view of the magazine appears rather like a railway shunting yard. All ratings working on 'Seaslug' have to wear safety helmets. *[MoD, RN, Official*

Bottom right: The control panel in the engine room of *HMS Fife.* *[MoD, RN, Official*

The bridge on the 'County' class destroyers is totally enclosed. The captain and navigating officer on the bridge of *HMS Hampshire*.

[MoD, RN, *Official*

HMS Fife undergoing trials in February 1966. Note the absence of portholes in the hull.

[MoD, RN, *Official*

A Life on the Ocean Wave

ANTHONY J. WATTS

HMS *Fearless* is one of the Royal Navy's two Amphibious Assault ships. With the Commando Carriers these vessels replace the old landing ships of the Amphibious Warfare Squadron. Each ship can operate a RM Commando or an infantry battalion (up to 700 troops).   *[Crown Copyright COI*

73

The Commando ships *Albion* and *Bulwark* also form part of the Navy's amphibious forces. These two ex-carriers carry a total of 20 helicopters. Here helicopter aircrew are briefed on board *HMS Bulwark*.

[Crown Copyright COI

While the helicopter crews receive their briefing, Marine Commandos are briefed elsewhere by a company commander.

[Crown Copyright COI

Up on the flight deck helicopters operate to deploy
and support the force of 700 commandos carried
by the *Bulwark*. Each 'Wessex V' helicopter can
transport a dozen fully armed commandos.

[Crown Copyright COI

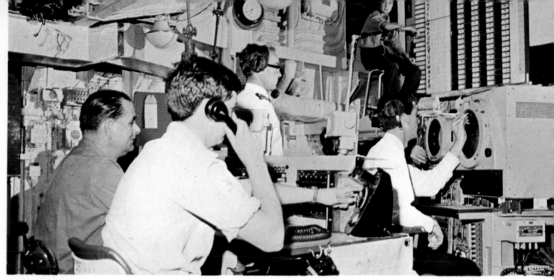

On the *Bulwark* the helicopter operations room keeps track of all the helicopters, noting all relevant information regarding the operation in progress.

[Crown Copyright COI

In addition to the Commandos the *Bulwark* and *Albion* also carry a Commando Battery, Royal Artillery, equipped with 105mm howitzers. These are transported and supplied by the helicopters, Here a 'Wessex' lifts off after having delivered a 105mm pack howitzer to a forward gun position for 29 Commando Light Regiment, Royal Artillery.

[Crown Copyright COI

New Destroyers of the Royal Navy

ANTHONY J. WATTS

Back in the early 1960's when designs for a new carrier (CVA-01) were put in hand for the Navy, it was decided that to meet the escort requirements of the vessel, a new class of destroyers would have to be designed. Previous Admiralty policy had been to design escorts with special tasks in mind (eg frigates like the 'Salisbury' class aircraft direction, 'Leopard' class anti-aircraft and 'Rothesay' class anti-submarine frigates), but when the 'Leander' class frigates were designed they were given a general purpose capability to meet any type of fleet escort duty. Although good sea boats, and for their size well armed, the 'Leander' class were not suitable for the escort requirements of the new carrier. Consequently a new type of general purpose escort vessel, the Type 82, was designed to meet the future needs of the Navy's carrier force. It must be said in passing that with the Labour Government's decision to phase out the carriers, a policy which although delayed by the Conservatives', is still a definite policy (to be implemented by the 1980's when the

last carrier *Ark Royal* is withdrawn from service), orders for three of the proposed new Type 82 vessels were cancelled. This left just one vessel, HMS *Bristol*. The *Bristol*, now undergoing trials certainly seems to be a first class vessel, but quite what role she will play in the Royal Navy, now that the carriers are to be withdrawn, is uncertain. She could of course, with her all round AA/AS capability and 30+ knots provide a first class escort for the new Through-Deck Cruiser, if one of these vessels is ever completed. The new surface-to-air missile SEA DART is carried aft together with a Limbo A/S mortar and a landing pad for a 'Lynx' A/S helicopter. Forward an IKARA mounting provides a further A/S weapon, while a 4.5in Mk 8 gun will provide a high rate of fire, presumably for support of troops ashore, for it is doubtful if warships will ever again come within range of a gunnery system when surface-to-surface missiles are available. Originally HMS *Bristol* was to have been fitted with an Anglo-Dutch 3D radar, but the project was cancelled, and she will now carry the normal air-warning radar. So far no plans have been made for the *Bristol* to carry EXOCET.

Now that the need for a fleet of large, highly sophisticated general purpose escorts has decreased, the Admiralty has designed a smaller and simpler, but no less powerful, type of destroyer needing fewer crew members (manpower has been one of the greatest problems in the Royal Navy over the last decade). A major factor in the design of the

An artist's impression of *HMS Bristol* as she would have appeared following the cancellation of the Anglo-Dutch 3D radar. In place of the 3D radar (which would have been housed in a large plastic dome on top of the bridge) the *Bristol* will now mount a double bedstead radar aerial.

[MoD, RN, Official

This artist's impression (the third that was drawn) depicts *HMS Bristol* as she will finally appear when completed. Note that two extra funnels have been added just aft of the mainmast. *[MoD, RN, Official*

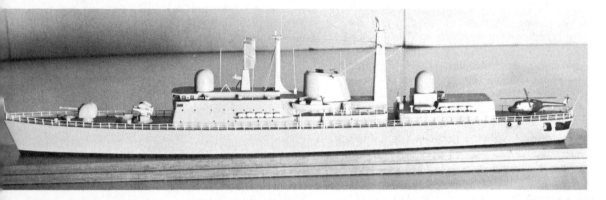

A model showing how *HMS Sheffield*, the first of the Type 42 destroyers, will appear when completed. *[MoD, RN, Official*

HMS Sheffield launched by Her Majesty the Queen at the Barrow yard of Vickers Ltd., on June 10, 1971. *[MoD, RN, Official*

new destroyers, the Type 42, of which five vessels are on order, was the adoption, following the successful trials in the frigate *Exmouth*, of the COGOG (COmbined Gas turbine Or Gas turbine) arrangement of gas turbines. Previously gas turbines have been used solely to provide short bursts of power and have been fitted in a COSAG (COmbined Steam And Gas turbine) arrangement in the 'County' class destroyers and adopted in HMS *Bristol*. The Type 42 lacks the long range IKARA A/S weapon of HMS *Bristol*, but is instead, equipped with a hangar to service and operate the 'Lynx' helicopter which will be armed with A/S torpedoes or air-to-surface missiles such as the French AS12, British HELLCAT or similar missile. The Type 42 also carries a SEA DART launcher and a 4.5 in Mk 8 gun, but as yet, no purely surface-to-surface missile.

The Dartmouth Cadet

SUB LTS R. CLARE & A. PISKA

Although naval colleges existed in one form or another throughout the early part of the 19th century, Naval Cadets, or 'volunteers first class', as they were called, received no formal instruction in professional or academic subjects. They went to sea at the age of thirteen to learn by practical experience. Those young officers who were fortunate enough to receive a College education were often frowned-on by their non-collegian seniors—and some captains even refused to have them onboard.

During the Crimean War HMS *Illustrious* was moored in Portsmouth Harbour and was used to train, not young naval officers, but young ratings. Under the command of Capt Robert Harris the training scheme proved to be a great success. Capt Harris was convinced that a similar training school was needed to train naval cadets, but despite his advice and the obvious success of the ratings' training school, the Admiralty decided that the idea of schooling was impractical—and they dismissed it. However, not to be so easily beaten, Capt Harris applied for permission to train his own son alongside the young seamen of the *Illustrious*. To his surprise, the Admiralty agreed that Cadet Harris should proceed with the course: such was its success that in 1857 a compulsory training scheme for all Cadets was ordered. The combined academic and professional training took place onboard the *Illustrious* in Portsmouth, and lasted for three months.

Soon the course outgrew the training ship and another vessel was ear-marked to take over: on January 1st, 1859, Capt Harris transferred his pennant to HMS *Britannia*—which had been laid up after the Crimean War. The course continued to grow under the guidance of Capt Harris—who, when he died in 1865, had left behind him the sort of training scheme that is perpetuated to-day in the Britannia Royal Naval College at Dartmouth. However, Portsmouth was a bad site for the training ship—she was moored in the unhealthy reaches of Haslar Creek—and after many complaints from anxious parents, the *Britannia* was moved to Portland, which also proved a bad choice due to the consistently poor weather conditions! (It was during her voyage to Portland that her sails were hoisted for the last time—with a fair wind down the Channel, she slipped the tug, whose best speed was six knots, and had soon overtaken it!) Finally, in 1863, the ship was ordered to move with the aid of a tug to the River Dart. This was to be her last move.

A year later, after an increase in the number of Cadets made conditions onboard the *Britannia* crowded, another ship, HMS *Hindostan*, was moored nearby to act as accommodation ship. In 1869 the larger

The Cadet's first sight of the College is the impressive frontage of the main building.

HM ships *Britannia* and *Hindostan* moored in the river Dart off Sandquay. The College buildings were erected in 1902 on the hillside above Sandquay.

Prince of Wales replaced the ageing *Britannia* and was re-named. There were now four entries of thirteen year old Cadets per year. The training took three months and the discipline was tough: corporal punishment was used regularly and a lesser punishment of several days on bread and water was sometimes implemented. In August 1869 the first scheme of competitive entry was introduced— it was to have a twice yearly entry of nominees and meant that more Cadets would be entered, but after a harder screening test. At the same time the course in the *Britannia* was extended to two years. Examinations in the various academic and professional subjects were held often and those Cadets who did not reach a satisfactory standard were given an 'Admiralty Warning', followed by discharge of those boys who did not improve. (A similar system of discharge exists today.)

As far back as 1863 it had been decided that a shore establishment should be re-introduced for the training of Cadets and by 1876 Dartmouth had been selected as the best of nine possible sites. However, it was not until 1896 that the final decision was taken to replace the two training ships. In 1900 construction work began on the main College building in the open fields above Sandquay— previously used by the Cadets for training and recreational purposes. The foundation stone was laid by King Edward VII in 1902 and the first Cadets moved into the buildings in 1905. Shortly afterwards, HMS *Hindostan*

was towed away and eleven years later HMS *Britannia* followed her to the shipbreakers— her precious copper being used for munitions.

Radical changes took place in Cadets' training at the turn of the century when Lord Selbourne and Adm Sir John Fisher recognised that a far more comprehensive academic and naval education was required. Cadets joined The Royal Naval College at Osborne on the Isle of Wight and studied there for two years before joining Dartmouth at the age of fifteen and completing a further two years training there. In 1913 a 'Special Entry' scheme was introduced to meet the increasing Fleet demands for Junior Officers. A small number of boys joined a Devonport-based training Cruiser straight from school at the age of eighteen. After eighteen months training these young Officers joined the Fleet with their Dartmouth-trained contemporaries.

The success of the scheme guaranteed its continuation—until 1939, when the Special Entry Cadets were sent to Dartmouth for basic shore training. They formed their own Division named after Adm Benbow and maintained an individual identity as 'Benbows' until 1955, when the two separate schemes were abolished and a single eighteen year old entry introduced. In 1914 the cadets were mobilised and found themselves at sea within two days. Osborne continued to train thirteen years olds throughout the war, but in 1920 drastic cuts were ordered in Government expenditure and Osborne College was closed, and its training task taken over by Dartmouth. Many cadets had to resign; their parents being repaid the fees which the Admiralty received from them for the naval education of their sons.

The Selbourne-Fisher scheme of entry continued to operate until 1948 and during the intervening years little change was made to the training plan—except as was necessary to keep abreast of a changing Navy. In 1942 the College came under direct attack from German bombers, and the seven junior terms of Cadets were evacuated to an orphanage in Bristol. The four senior terms remained at Dartmouth until 1943, when the College was reformed at Eaton Hall near Chester. The College buildings survived the bombing well, and the buildings were used by various allied units during the war years. The task of Cadet training did not begin again here until 1946.

Then, in 1948, came the most important change of all: the entry system was so altered that 'no boy is prevented from competing (for entry) by reason of his social status, schooling or financial standing'. Soon afterwards all fees for upkeep and tuition were abolished, the age of entry was raised to sixteen, and the training time reduced to six terms. However, the change did not attract the numbers of candidates required and after a study made in 1952, Parliament was informed that in future all Cadets would enter the Service at eighteen. The last of the sixteen year olds left the College in 1955 and the subsequent new entries joined for seven terms—including two cruises in the Dartmouth Training Squadron. After three terms the Cadets were promoted Midshipmen and, on passing out, Sub-Lieutenants—after which they were appointed to the Fleet for further training.

The entire system of Officer entry and training was reviewed in 1958 and the scheme that exists today began in September 1960. General List Officers join at the age of $17\frac{1}{2}$, with five GCE passes, including two at 'A' level. The first year of training is almost entirely professional—with three months in the Dartmouth Training Squadron. The second year of training sees the young Officer at sea in the Fleet as a Midshipman. After passing the Midshipman's Examination Board, executive and supply branch officers return to Dartmouth as Acting Sub-Lieutenants for a year's academic traning. The engineer Officers

Cadet's training begins here.

Waterborne activities play an important part in the Cadet's training.

go to the Royal Naval Engineering College at Manadon for a degree course in engineering. Supplementary List (Short Service) Officers who join Dartmouth with five 'O' levels, as Seamen, carry out a similar training scheme to their General List contemporaries, but do not return to the College for an Academic year. Instead, they are appointed to ships in the Fleet in complement billets. Short Service Aircrew Cadets spend only two terms at the

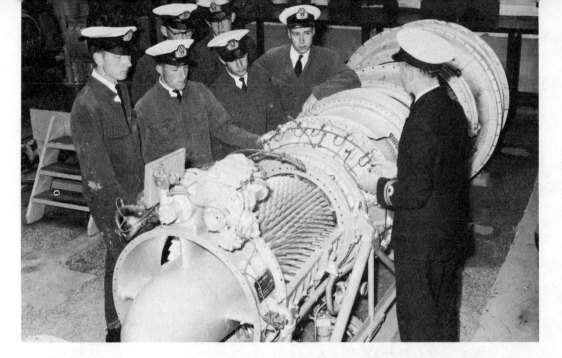

The Navy's propulsion system for the future—the Gas Turbine.

Cadets undergoing professional instruction. Navigational training onboard the minesweeper attached to the College.

Sport plays an important part in the lives of Cadets at the College. Here the 1st XV are at home to a crack West Country side.

College before beginning intensive flying training elsewhere.

An increasing number of young men now join the Navy through one of the Graduate Entry schemes: either as 'Direct Entries' (DEG) on graduating, or as University Cadet Entries (UCEs) who are acting midshipmen and paid as such whilst taking their degree course; their tuition fees also being paid by the MOD. The UCEs are expected to undergo a minimum of three weeks naval training a year with the fleet during their university vacations and on graduating join the direct entry graduates in completing three months basic naval training at Dartmouth. Graduates with teaching experience join as instructor officers and on completion of the Dartmouth training are appointed as Lieutenants to the Royal Navy's shore establishments to fill

teaching posts. Some go to larger fleet units as Meteorological officers.

General List Cadets with the necessary academic qualifications may also be selected to take a degree course after their first two years training. Instead of returning to the college as Sub-Lieutenants they go to the university of their choice to begin studies. Today there are nearly 626 Officers Under Training—who may have entered via any one of eighteen possible entry schemes!

Throughout the years, as faces, ages and methods have changed, one thing has remained constant, the Aim of Dartmouth training. A recent Captain of the College summed it up, ".... to train young men to Act and React Instinctively as Officers." More is demanded of young Officers to-day than has ever been the case before as the sailors who serve under them are more intelligent, and the work they do more exacting. Consequently every Officer must be totally professional if he is to lead and command the respect of his men. The Britannia Royal Naval College has now a correspondingly more challenging task to perform. Nearly 100 Staff Officers and Civilian Lecturers control the training plan—attempting to achieve the fine balance of effort that ensures efficiency, fitness and happiness in the trainees .... always remaining within the limits of the Aim.

The Cadet of 1971 has, on average, six months ashore at the College in which to acquire a sound theoretical knowledge of all the departments of a modern warship. The syllabus is broad: seamanship, navigation (including astro navigation), engineering (mechanical and electrical), gunnery, undersea warfare, communications, man-management, supply and secretariat, naval history, air warfare, amphibious operations, damage control and parade training—being just some of the headings. The professional course is virtually common to all Cadets—though future short service aircrew and International Cadets from the navies of Libya, Iran, Malaysia and Singapore have special courses. 'Bull' is almost dead in the Navy now, but it is still realised that the self discipline and

Practical leadership training on Dartmoor. A cadet from the Royal Malaysian Navy crosses a 'deep ravice'.

personal pride and self confidence acquired on the parade ground make parade training a very valuable and essential part of the syllabus. To achieve the required standard of drill new entry Cadets spend at least one hour a day on the parade ground and at the end of their fourth week in the College they are examined by the Parade Training Officer; success qualifies a Cadet for his first shore leave at the end of the sixth week—few fail!

Much of the Cadets' training is done, perhaps sub-consciously, by the Sub-Lieutenants in their third year of training in the Navy. They have completed their year in the Fleet as Midshipmen and return to Dartmouth as Seamen or Supply Officers on the General List to study mathematics, general science, history, economics and languages at a tertiary level. The science course broadens the Sub-Lieutenants' knowledge of the principles behind much of the complicated electrical and mechanical equipment in service with the Fleet and topics include oceanography, meteorology, 'computers', and nuclear physics. The Humanities course acts as a counterbalance and the choice of subjects open to

Officers under training, includes 'A Study of Peace and War', 'Naval History', 'Contemporary Affairs' and a choice of one of seven Foreign Languages—from Russian to Malay. They bring with them a new-found experience and self confidence, which combined with the small age gap tends to make them better equipped to teach the Cadets by example than anyone else in the College: a point made by Capt. A. G. Tait DSC, the last Captain of the College, in his welcoming address to the Third Year: '... Cadets assume that the Captain and the Commander and the Director of Studies know nothing; that their Divisional Officers and Tutors know just a little more than that and that Sub-Lieutenants know everything.'! Every Cadet is thus allocated to a 'Guidance Sub-Lieutenant', or 'Sea-daddy', who amongst other things, is able to tell his Cadets salty, hairy stories of the sea after his own experience of the recently completed Midshipman's Year! By discussing each of his Cadet's general progress at regular intervals and by pointing out, unpatronisingly, their faults, the Guidance Sub-Lieutenant can make a new entry feel at ease, and will almost certainly be able to contribute to the Cadet's general naval training.

A day in the life of a Dartmouth Cadet illustrated in the form of a wheel showing relative times allocated to each activity.

Every Cadet is allocated to one of five Divisions—named after famous Admirals; Jellicoe, Blake, Hawke, Cunningham and St Vincent. Each Division is headed by an Officer of Lieutenant-Commander's rank whose job it is to decide the course that divisional life will take. He will supervise the Cadet's training and administrative needs and will ensure that every Cadet does his bit for the Division—on the sports field, on the river, or in some other useful way: always watching for signs of weakness so that early steps may be taken to reject unsuitable characters—he will go out of his way to assist a Cadet who finds some part of the course difficult to master. Each Cadet is also allocated a Civilian Tutor who will assist him if he finds problems with the academic training. The Tutors report on the Cadets in their sets—so providing a double-check on the Cadet's progress through the College. Most Tutors are permanent staff, thus they also fulfil the valuable task of continuity, since Divisional Officers remain in the College for only 2 years. The most important Sub-Lieutenant, as far as the new entry is concerned, is the 'Divisional Sub-Lieutenant' who is chosen especially for his qualities of leadership and personal bearing to be in charge of the Cadet Division—perhaps 50 or 60 Cadets. He is directly responsible to the Cadet Divisional Officer for ensuring that the Division is efficiently organised and that the Cadets' domestic standards are high—for example, stowage of kit, smartness of turnout etc. The Cadets tend to view the Divisional Sub-Lieutenant with a little awe and will probably learn a lot from him that will be of considerable value in their early years in the Service.

Awake at 0600, the New Entry Cadet will attend 'Early Morning Activities' every morning, except Sunday, for the first 6 weeks of his career—morse flashing, physical training, swimming or parade training will occupy half an hour before breakfast. This meal will often be a hurried affair, snatched in the modern, cafeteria style dining hall, after which the Cadet hurries to make up his bunk, square off his cabin and be ready to begin 'After Breakfast Activities' at 0745. On three days a week this will be 'Divisions'—a traditional ceremony in the Navy, akin to the Army's Parade—when the Cadets fall in by divisions on the parade ground to be inspected by their Divisional Officers. Then prayers are said and and the ceremony of 'Colours' takes place when the White Ensign is hoisted on the mast, to the strains of the National Anthem (played by the Royal Marine Band stationed at the College). Finally the divisions march past, smartly in line, heads swivelled to the right in salute to the Captain. At 0830 the Cadet is ready to begin the day's instruction! Six one-hour periods every day, except Wednesday and the weekends, including one or two periods of physical training, make up the formal training time. Breaks in the routine occur at intervals: several days are spent flying in the College Flight's 'Wasp' Helicopter or in one of the 'Chipmunk' Trainer aircraft maintained at Roborough Airfield, near Plymouth. Two or three days are spent at sea in the minesweeper attached to the College—to give Cadets their first experience of practical navigation and seamanship. Day visits are arranged to such places as The Plymouth Planetarium—for a look at the best known navigational aids; to a small arms range; and to the firefighting school in HMS *Raleigh*. The Cadets will later find pertinent questions in their examination papers on matters they should have noted during these visits.

The less formal part of a Cadet's general training will be covered by his Divisional Officer during specially nominated periods. Subjects covered include: 'Behaviour at Cocktail Parties', 'Service Letter Writing', 'Dress Ashore' and 'Leadership'. Cadets are also expected to prepare and deliver talks lasting between ten and fifteen minutes on subjects of their choice. Divisional Officers also keep a close watch on the Cadets' 'Activity Logs' which are completed weekly and contain brief descriptions of a Cadet's sporting or river activities for every day of the week. They give Cadets the chance to express their thoughts and opinions in writing and so prepare them for the task of Journal writing that they will encounter in the Fleet as Midshipmen. Not all the Cadets' training takes place within the College: essential character building exercises on the moors and in the countryside around Dartmouth are included in the syllabus and occur at regular intervals. Every weekend one or other of the Divisions draw camping gear and embark on an expedition into the wilds of Devon (often travelling by boat up the Dart) to 'defend' some imaginary installation from attack by 'aggressors', or to practise map reading in an orienteering exercise. Cadets are chosen to lead teams of five or six of their contemporaries during these exercises, so 'taking charge' of a group of men and attempting to achieve an objective for possibly the first time in their lives.

After a full day of professional training the Cadet is almost worn out by 1645, when the recreational period beings! Such are the facilities at the College that a Cadet may take up any sport or activity he cares to mention. However, there is seldom sufficient time to take up more than one or two, because the Cadet is required to spend a minimum of two afternoons a week on the River Dart in one of the many boats maintained by the College for practical seamanship training. Only by constant practice will he gain sufficient expertise to be able to pass a demanding handling test in each class of boat. When he later joins the Fleet he will meet most of the types of boat in use at the College and it is important that a young man of the sea should be proficient in their use. Those Cadets who are fortunate to be good enough, may find that they have been selected to play for one of the College sports teams—an honour indeed, but hard work. They will be expected to train on two afternoons a week and will then defend the high reputation of the College against crack West Country teams on two other afternoons. Clearly the remaining two afternoons have to be devoted to river work and so fond hopes of skiing in Norway, cruising in one of the College yachts to France, flying in a 'Chipmunk' to gain a pilot's licence or joining the famous Britannia Beagles on a fast-moving chase across the countryside nearby, are finally dashed!

Divisional life is taken seriously at the College—both to extract the right spirit from the Cadets and to demonstrate to them the value of the Navy's 'Divisional System'. Competition is fostered whenever possible, as, for example, in the case of the Inter-Divisional Sports Trophy which is awarded at the end of each term to the Division that has been the most successful at a number of sports and activities—ranging from the Rugby Knockout to the Bosun Dinghy racing series. Other mass events such as the Sailing Regatta and 'Away all Boats' (an exercise in seamanship, against the clock) are popular and victories are celebrated with much gusto in the local taverns! Once a term each Division holds its own mess dinner, to which a distinguished guest is invited—usually a senior Naval Officer—and for possibly the first time the Cadet realises that there is a gentlemanly side to his chosen career! The whole Division sits down to eat in the traditional manner—Divisional Officers, Tutors, Sub-Lieutenants and Cadets all enjoy the meal together and afterwards speeches are made by the Divisional Sub-Lieutenant and the guest of honour. The correct procedures and traditions are thus taught pleasantly and painlessly! Apart from these occasions, social life is virtually nil as there is not sufficient time in a Cadet's routine for any other organised functions during the term, except for the two end of term Balls which are open to Cadets.

Cadets are expected to perform various College duties each term, as members of the Divisional Guard, as coxswain of the Duty Motor Cutter on the river, as members of the Colours and Sunset flag party or perhaps as Commander's Messenger. However trivial the duty two things are important: firstly, for many of the Cadets, the duty will be the very first taste of responsibility, with penalties to be awarded for failure; secondly, the prestige of the Division is at stake if things go wrong— very often the scorn of his fellows is the worst punishment a Cadet could suffer! Throughout the Cadets' training they are learning to carry out simple tasks correctly so that the greater responsibilities that they will have in the Fleet will be second nature to them.

To be able to relax for short periods becomes vitally important to Cadets after they have concentrated hard on their studies during the long days at Dartmouth. Culturally, the Britannia Society of Music and the Arts, caters for most tastes by arranging regular performances by well known artists in such widely differing fields as Folk Music and Ballet Dancing; an annual College Play that is entered for the Inter Command Drama Competition; an annual College Revue and the provision of facilities for giving music lessons on instruments from the piano to the guitar. It is very easy for Cadets to forget the world outside after the first few days within the organisation and bustle of the College so interludes spent relaxing to good music or singing become very welcome! A NAAFI canteen is provided for the use of Cadets every evening—only beer is sold, but a television and billiards table are provided for general amusement.

With the basic theoretical knowledge under his belt the Cadet is ready to put ideas into practice at the end of his second term in the College. They join one of the three Frigates in the 'Dartmouth Training Squadron', whose sole function is to take Cadets to sea for three months' sea training during their third term in the Navy. During 'flag-showing' cruises to Scandinavia or the Mediterranean. Cadets live onboard the frigates of the Squadron on messdecks that are identical to those used by ratings in ships at sea—in fact the ships of the Squadron are deliberately under-complemented with seaman ratings and the Cadets are employed chipping and painting; running the boats; on the fo'c'sle when anchoring and generally all over the ship where they will learn, through first hand experience, the basic practical aspects of their future career. As Cadet Officer of the Watch, an 18 year old will be allowed to give the orders to the helmsman and the engine room that will manoeuvre his £5 million ship into station less than 100 yards from other ships in the Squadron ... the Captain will be right beside him—ready to intervene in the event of drama, but the knowledge gained by this first hand experience is immense!

With the first year of training behind them the Cadets become Midshipmen and leave Dartmouth for the ships of the Fleet. Meanwhile, the cycle has already started again: new faces—new ideas—new methods, the College is constantly changing to keep pace not only with a changing Navy, but also with a changing society. The accent is on professionalism and anyone may volunteer to have a go and those who are successful leave Dartmouth as young Naval Officers. The Aim of the College will always remain the same; 'to act and react instinctively as Officers'.

Life in a Polaris Submarine

Lt-Cdr A. J. R. WATSON RN

The submarine has been at sea for some time now, and having reached our patrol area is cruising stealthily through it. Even onboard only a handful of people are aware of our position, and of them the Captain and Navigating Officer alone know the limits of our area and where we are going next. As far as our families and friends are concerned we have simply disappeared for a couple of months because, to avoid compromising our position, we will be dived and maintaining radio silence for the entire patrol.

Life onboard has by now settled down to a well established basic routine which everyone has adopted to meet his individual requirements. To answer the question which all our families must have asked at one time or another—"What do you actually *do* all day?" —is quite difficult within the bounds of security and without boring them in the sheer technicalities of our own particular job. As the submarine is, generally speaking, manned on a three watch basis, there is a considerable part of each day during which we are not actively involved with our job, and even after discounting time spent on such necessary activities as sleeping and eating there is still quite a lot of free time on our hands. Perhaps the easiest place to begin is by considering our environment and the domestic side of our way of life, before looking at how we tackle the specific problems of being a Polaris Submarine.

By normal submarine standards living conditions for the 150 people onboard are palatial; each person having a permanent and exclusive bunk space even if the rest of the accommodation is communal. Here, at least, is privacy where one can read or sleep without affecting anyone else. Otherwise conditions are not unlike living in a crowded railway sleeper—fine providing everyone is not trying to do the same thing simultaneously, but rather frustrating when the amenities are overwhelmed by numbers. In the living spaces the overall impressions are of peace and quiet with the only obvious sounds being due to the ventilation. In fact it is sometimes quite difficult to believe we are at sea at all, for usually the submarine's motion is so slight as to be unnoticeable.

As with most basically routine ways of life,

CUTAWAY OF A POLARIS SUBMARINE

1 Rudders & Hydroplanes
2 Motor room
3 Main machinery space
4 Machinery control panels
5 Auxiliary motors
6 Reactor compartment
7 Missile hatches
8 Missile compartment
9 Control room
10 Senior ratings mess
11 Dining hall
12 Forward hydroplanes
13 Junior ratings' recreation space
14 Torpedo tubes.

[MoD, RN, Official

food assumes an importance beyond its intrinsic value and it can have a tremendous influence for good or ill on our morale. On the whole causes for complaint are few as our fridges and provision stores have been carefully stocked to give us both good quality, and variety, as we eat our way into them. Only a very fussy eater would be unable to find satisfaction from at least one of the choices available at each meal. Exercise facilities onboard are virtually non-existent, so the problem of dieting is one that has at least to be considered by almost everyone. It becomes an obsession for a few people who contrive to lose a lot of weight by resorting to dramatic changes in their eating habits. However, for the majority, a natural reduction in appetite and alcohol intake are sufficient to maintain their status quo. It is certainly rare for anyone to put on weight significantly during a patrol.

Beer consumption is modest due to both commensense and lack of stowage space onboard. It is probably appropriate to men-

Junior ratings bunk space   [MoD, RN, Official

tion here the rather unglamorous, but inevitable problem of gash. Liquid waste is easily disposed of by collecting it in various tanks and pumping it overboard when safe to do so. Solids, on the other hand, are dealt with by compacting them into sheet metal cannisters that we assemble onboard. They are then discharged overboard from an ejector —a process rather like firing miniature torpedoes.

Our atmosphere presents an unusual problem as it is now quite independent of normal air supplies, and we require a lot of special equipment both to maintain its required level of oxygen and to remove such gases as carbon monoxide and carbon dioxide, which are not only normal by-products of our way of life, but also lethal in quite small concentrations. Our oxygen is normally produced by electrolysis from sea water, and the harmful gases removed by other chemical processes. By the time all the air conditioning and filtering have been taken into account our resulting atmosphere is cleaner, if not quite as pure, as that existing in an average town. To live in it seems dry but otherwise quite unremarkable, although our families are forever complaining that we and our clothes smell of 'Nuclear Submarine' even after only a few hours onboard. Like most ship smells it is a bit indefinable, but is probably a mixture of oil, steam, hot machinery, cooking, warm electronics and cigarette smoke. Another minor oddity in our lives is that there is quite an extensive list of prohibited articles from the atmosphere point of view, ranging from aerosol sprays (which are usually worked by freon) through most paints and glues down to metal polish. All of them give off harmful products in an enclosed environment such as ours. Even shoe polish is discouraged, if not absolutely banned, which is one reason why sandals and artificial leather shoes are so commonly worn at sea.

Whilst many people will have brought along a variety of hobbies to keep them occupied, inevitably the most universal spare time activities are reading and watching films. Reading requirements are easily satisfied for, in addition to the official library, there are paperbacks and old magazines everywhere which—if not privately owned—have found their way into a multitude of unofficial libraries around the submarine. We are not exactly lacking in films either as we have more than enough onboard to show a different one every day of the patrol. The Base Film Library will have reserved its most recent releases for us, and the remainder of our selection varies from the fairly new to those nearly old enough to be shown on TV. The principle showing of any film is in the evening, and any watchkeepers get a chance to see it when it is repeated the following afternoon. Really good films sometimes even get a midnight performance as well. This concentrated film-going is excellent escapism and entertainment for ourselves even if—as is quite often the case—we have seen the film before. But, it is the despair of many of our families, who find that we have almost invariably seen all but the very latest films that they think they would like to be taken to see.

The submarine's newspaper has run to several editions by now. Budding journalists and cartoonists are usually at a premium, but the editors manage to produce something rather like a mixture between *Punch* and *Private Eye* which gives everyone a good laugh. The theme is almost invariably humorous, and in fact any edition is usually an accurate reflection of the mood of the moment, which is so inexplicable to anyone who doesn't know the background to the incidents or characters involved. Even though it does not appear in the newspaper, genuine news does reach us in the form of a news bulletin on the broadcast system, and once a week we get local news of the Base and Helensburgh area which has been compiled by the Off Crew.

For general entertainment records and tapes are relayed round the living spaces on the SRE system. Quizzes are also very popular and on this patrol we are repeating our previously successful University Challenge type knock-out challenge with about a dozen teams competing.

Although, of course, we cannot contact our families, they can at least send us a 40-word Familygram once a week, which goes some way towards letting us know what is happening at home. Before we sailed we gave our families a stock of special forms which they will now be posting at suitable intervals to the Off Crew Office in the Base. There they will be processed and sent on for transmission on the broadcast to us. Editing, as such, is usually unnecessary, unless someone has not followed the rules; but bad news is suppressed and dealt with, if possible, according to the instructions that we have left behind for such contingencies. As there is absolutely nothing that we can do about it at sea except worry, such news is best kept from us until shortly before we get back, when there is a chance to adjust to it before an otherwise happy homecoming.

Night and day are relatively unimportant to us, although from our domestic routine it is obvious which is which. An actual impression of night is formed by switching the passageways and Control Room to red lighting at night, but this is more of a precaution to preserve our night vision in case we have to go to periscope depth than for any psychological reason. Days of the week have little significance either, although some events such as Captain's Rounds and Church repeat themselves on a weekly basis. Once we have settled into our patrol routine the passage of time is deceptive, and because we are such an enclosed

Junior ratings dining hall   *[MoD, RN, Official*

community it soon seems absolutely ages since we sailed. The days themselves pass quickly, but time seems to stand still. Then, suddenly, we find ourselves in the last few days of the patrol, and despite the extra work involved in preparing for our return, the days begin to drag like the end of a school term.

To see how the submarine actually functions it is perhaps logical to begin aft in the machinery spaces without which we would not be a going concern in any shape or form. Unlike the rest of the submarine, it is undeniably warm in the machinery spaces. The other dominant feature of working there is that the necessity to fit a vast amount of equipment into relatively small spaces makes the problem of accessibility quite acute at times. It is an area of contrasts. At one end of the scale there is the sophisticated modern technology of the reactor system and its instrumentation, and at the other the rather traditional propulsion machinery.

Nothing would appear further removed from machinery spaces than the Medical Department, but in fact the bulk of their routine work is concerned with health physics (i.e. reactor chemistry and radiation monitoring), and atmosphere control; tasks which involve the medical staff in many hours of sampling and analysing in and around the machinery spaces. Fortunately, their more conventional medical skills are not usually much in demand, but it is certainly very reassuring to know that the Medical Officer and his staff are around, as it is unlikely that we could get any external medical assistance for some time if a serious illness or accident occurred. Even though the medical facilities onboard are naturally limited, in such an eventuality they hope to be able to at least treat a patient sufficiently to stabilise his condition until better medical facilities are available.

The control room of the submarine is quite roomy with the central pillars of the huge periscopes, and dual diving controls which resemble those of an aircraft. Just off the control room is the Navcentre where the two SINS (Ships Inertial Navigation System) and a variety of supporting navigation equipment enable us to have a continousuly available position to feed to the Polaris Fire Control computers. Like all man-made devices, SINS are not perfect, and with time they gradually develop errors due to a number of factors such as minor imperfections in their gyros.

The recreation space [MoD, RN, Official

The watch in the Navcentre are concerned with monitoring many aspects of the SINS performance, both relative to each other and to occasional fixes obtained from one of our Navaids. After a while this monitoring enables the various SINS errors to be determined and the results used to reset the SINS to a correct starting point.

Two decks below the Navcentre is the Missile Control Centre (MCC) where another watch is performing routine missile and fire control tests. In normal circumstances it is probably the most peaceful and clinical compartment in the submarine. In common with the other particularly sensitive areas onboard, access is limited to the few people who have a need to go there. It is from the MCC that a Missile Countdown will be controlled, and—as its name implies—it contains the fire control computers and other equipment necessary to prepare the missiles for launching. The fire control computers are perpetually solving the fire control problem for each of our missiles to engage its target as soon as its guidance system gyros are spun up and aligned.

The specifially Polaris areas are completed by the Missile Compartment (MC) where yet another watch are continuously monitoring the missiles themselves and their environment. It is the largest single compartment in the submarine and contains not only the missile tubes and launcher equipment but also some offices and stores that are too bulky to be stowed anywhere else. Apart from a small area where the missiles are monitored and the launching functions controlled, the MC is normally open for general use. In fact there are some nice secluded spaces between the tubes where people can read, paint, or make models, etc. For keen exercisers the bicycling machine can be found there too. Otherwise nowhere is the physical security of the Polaris Weapon System so obvious or necessary, and there are locks, interlocks and alarms on anything that is important or potentially hazardous. Perhaps because the missiles in their tubes are normally hidden from our view, the close proximity of nuclear weapons and

powerful rocket motors is easy enough to live with, and as a result the atmosphere in the MC is far from sinister.

To get us on patrol in the first place required an enormous amount of hard work on the part of the Base, the other crew and ourselves. The availability of scarce or supposedly unobtainable stores verged on the miraculous at times. Sometimes all the known, and a few unknown, stops have been pulled out to get us away on time. Now it is entirely up to us. The submarine has been designed and stored to fulfil its role for somewhat longer than the duration of this patrol, and in the face of a large number of possible defects. All important systems and equipments have a certain amount of built in redundancy, but it is possible to conceive that an unusual combination of defects could prejudice our ability to complete the patrol. In these circumstances, with no possibility of outside advice or material assistance, we have to make

Checking battery temperatures on number 3 deck. A general view of a junior ratings bunk space area.
[MoD RN, Official

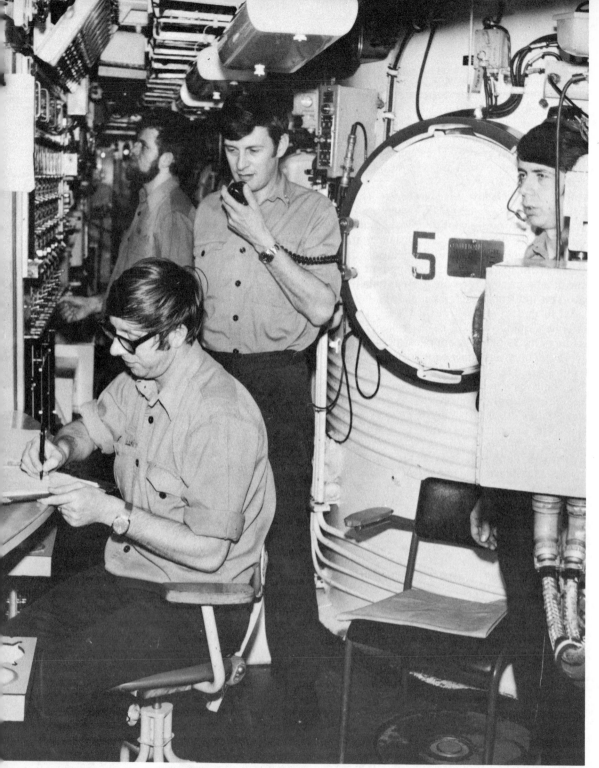

The Polaris missile compartment.

[MoD, RN, Official

Preparing lunch in the galley.

[MoD, RN, Official

do with what we have at hand, and it is then that the full measure of our training, experience and native ingenuity has to come into its own. Professional pride alone will ensure that we will sort ourselves out somehow, if it is humanly possible. It is perhaps true to say that nowhere in the Navy are the disciplines of readiness and self-reliance more necessary than here in a Polaris submarine.

What of our immediate thoughts? Mostly these will be of our families and friends. Many of us with small children, in particular, will be wondering how they have changed and grown up while we have been away. For

a few there will be thoughts of seeing a new baby for the first time. We are all sustained by thoughts of our homecoming. Quite a number of families will be on the jetty to meet us although they know that we will, at first, only be able to see them very briefly before a host of immediate jobs, such as connecting up shore supplies and preparing to shut down the reactor, must be attended to.

Just now we have a lot to look forward to apart from our actual return. A couple of days after we get back the traumatic process of crew changing will come to a head, and we will hand over the submarine to the other

95

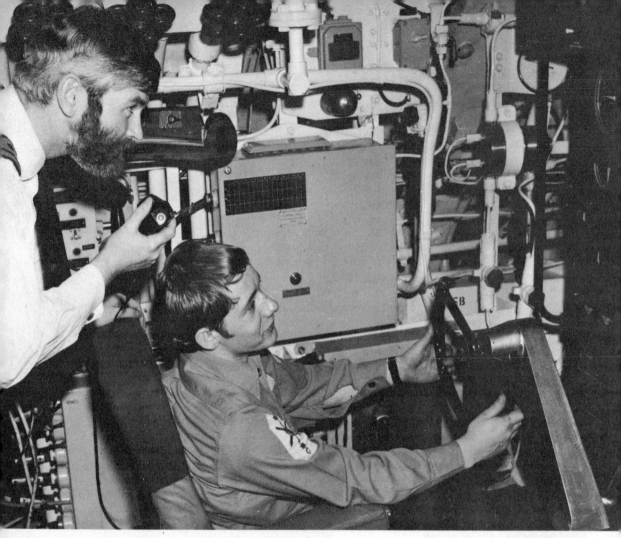

The Officer of the watch and planesman in the control room.   *[MoD, RN, Official*

crew. Then we will be free for the four days of our patrol week-end and with the prospect of becoming Off Crew. It is nice to imagine our freedom from responsibility and the claustrophobic effects of living so completely on top of our job with absolutely no escape from it. After the Patrol week-end we will help the other crew to prepare for their next patrol and see them safely away before taking our Main Leave.

After that the tone of our thoughts will begin to swing the other way, and as we return from our leave to do refresher training thoughts of the submarine's return will increasingly loom in our minds. Having just got used to having us properly home again our families will have to begin to adjust to another impending parting. For us, the prospect of that on top of the hard work and domestically unsettling time of the maintenance period before our next patrol is not pleasant. In fact, as the time draws near, we know that it will be a tremendous relief to sail, and we will find ourselves actively looking forward to the patrol almost as much as we are now looking forward to getting home—but for rather different reasons.

Replenishment at Sea

ANTHONY J. WATTS

As early as 1906 experiments were being conducted to explore the feasibility of underway replenishment. Already oil-fired warships were under construction, and in 1905 the tanker *Petroleum* was acquired and refitted with experimental equipment with which she carried out the first successful refuelling of a warship at sea. For the trials, the *Petroleum* was towed behind the battleship *Hindustan* at a distance of about 800ft. From a strong wire hawser suspended between the two vessels hung a number of chain straps supporting a 5in bronze fuel pipe. This pipe ran the length of the tanker, and was suspended from a rail by more chain straps which ran on rollers along the rail until it reached the bows of the tanker, where it passed to the straps on the wire hawser. Known as the stirrup method the system was clumsy and took hours to rig.

Gradually the equipment was improved, and by 1910 more powerful pumps had increased the rate of flow. The tanker was also able to replenish a warship from either the bow position or the stern. Breaks frequently occurred in the bronze pipe as a result of the high pumping pressures, or from strain when the two vessels suddenly veered away from each other, and when speeds varied.

At the outbreak of World War I the Royal Fleet Auxiliary (RFA) possessed a fleet of eight ships which increased during the war to 87 vessels, the majority of which were oil tankers. This rapid increase in establishment, with the emphasis on oil tankers, was brought about by an almost complete changeover from coal-burning to oil-fired warships. After the war approximately twenty deep-sea freighting tankers ('*War*' and '*01*' classes) were retained, a number of fast escort oilers ('Leaf' class) and some small tankers for use as fleet attendants; the remainder being returned to commercial ownership.

With the reduction in Naval Estimates during the 1920's, and with bases scattered throughout the world, little was done to build up the RFA, or to improve methods of Replenishment At Sea (RAS). Not until the middle 1930's was any real progress made in re-equipping the RFA. Then in 1936 a committee was set up to investigate and report on the future requirements of the RFA. The report, presented in 1938, envisaged a situation in which possibly as a result of air attack, the Admiralty would be unable to rely on its overseas bases, and would instead, be entirely reliant on mobile support afloat. Unfortunately World War II began before many of the recommendations put forward by the committee could be implemented.

As part of the plan for improving the facilities provided by the RFA a new cargo ship, the *Reliant*, was bought from her commercial owners and converted into a stores issuing

Multi-ship replenishment-at-sea operations, such as the one illustrated here, are one of the rarer types of supply exercise practised by vessels of the RFA. The vessels in the above illustration are from left to right *Retainer* (ammunition supply), *Galatea* (frigate), *Reliant* (air stores supply vessel), *Hermes* (carrier), *Tideflow* (replenishment tanker), and *Minerva* (frigate).   [MoD, RN, Official

vessel; the first of the new 'Dale' class of tankers was delivered as well as a number of coastal and ocean going store carriers. The new supply vessels, apart from the tankers which were equipped with facilities for RAS using the new derrick method, were mainly used to transport stores and supplies from Britain to overseas bases.

During 1937 important experiments led to the introduction of the derrick method of refuelling involving the supply tanker and warship steaming on parallel courses a set distance apart, and requiring a high degree of accuracy in station keeping. The vessels were prevented from veering away from each other by double 8in manilla springs. Refuelling was carried out from a standard mercantile derrick sited in the waist of the tanker. From this derrick a light steel line carried a $3\frac{1}{2}$in bronze fuel pipe to the warship. The main problem encountered with the new system was the interaction of the resulting bow waves between the two vessels. These gave rise to a powerful suction effect which tended to draw the two vessels together.

In 1942 two German oilers sent to replenish the *Bismarck* were captured. After closely studying the methods used for replenishment on board these tankers a number of improvements were made to the derrick system. One of the most important alterations involved the fuel hose. The Germans had been using rubber hose and this was found to be far superior to

the bronze pipe used by the Royal Navy. Owing to shortage of materials it was not possible to effect an immediate changeover from bronze to rubber. To increase the range of escorts a number of commercial tankers were fitted for carrying out replenishment and were sailed with the convoys. Those that carried the rubber hose and were fitted for fuelling astern had far greater success with RAS operations than those equipped for fuelling abeam. In spite of the fact that escorts found it difficult to pick up the rubber hose and maintain station astern of a tanker, once accomplished, refuelling could often be carried out in the comparatively short time of two hours and in adverse weather conditions. Abeam refuelling was still only in its infancy at this stage of World War II, and in cases where it was attempted from the commercial tankers sailing in the convoys, RAS was found to be more or less impossible, unless the sea was dead calm. Gradually, however, the bronze hoses were replaced by 5in rubber hose and other improvements such as the fitting of two or more sets of samson posts in the tanker's well decks greatly facilitated the task of RAS. With the new samson posts, which supported a much longer derrick, extra block and tackle enabled the hose to be hung in two or more troughs instead of the single trough used previously. This greatly eased the strain on the fuel pipe and helped to reduce breakages whilst fuelling

After the Second World War the jackstay was adapted for refuelling. Here the new replenishment tanker *Olna* supplies the carrier *Eagle* (now awaiting scrapping) with fuel. *[MoD, RN, Official*

The supply tanker *Wave Victor* refuelling a warship during exercise Main Brace in October 1953. The refuelling derricks of the 'Wave' class were originally used on old battleships to support the anti-torpedo nets round the hull.

[MoD, RN, Official]

was in progress. The two or more sets of samson posts also enabled a tanker to carry out refuelling from more than one point, so speeding up the process of RAS.

Other successful experiments were carried out with a self-tensioning winch on board the tanker *Grey Ranger.* The introduction of the new winch greatly eased the task of the winchman, and made transferring light loads at sea much safer.

During 1944 planning went ahead for the formation of a British Pacific Fleet (BPF). The need for an extensive logistic fleet to support the BPF operating far in advance of its main bases, was put forward by the Combined Chiefs of Staff. They stated that the BPF should be fully self-supporting as regards supplies. The Americans had already amassed a wealth of experience in operating a Fleet Train such as the Admiralty proposed to form. Every week a convoy would leave the United States for one of the forward bases in the Far East where the Fleet Train would replenish with supplies from the convoy. The Fleet Train would then sail for a pre-arranged rendezvous with the Task Forces about 100 miles from the battle front. Then at two or three day intervals groups of the Task Force would pull out from the operations area, replenish and return, where they would relieve another group in need of replenishment.

Having observed the success of the American RAS operations, which kept their fleets in the battle zone for months on end, the Admiralty concluded that the only way the BPF could operate as an effective unit would be to adopt the same system for replenishment. The main difficulty from the Navy's point of view was in finding sufficient merchant ships to serve as supply vessels, and crews to man them. The only possible source of shipping with crews available, were those vessels already employed in bringing vital imports to the United Kingdom. With great reluctance the Ministry of War Transport released a number of these vital vessels for use as Fleet Supply ships; they were not adequate in numbers for the Navy's needs, but they were all that could be spared.

In December 1944 it had been estimated that a total of six naval store issuing ships would be required to support the BPF, but by

A typical day's stores required for the carrier *Eagle* in 1956. Rum is no longer issued to *HM* warships.

[MoD, RN, Official

August 1945 only two ('Fort' class) were on station. Similarly of the 10 victualling store issuing ships required, only seven were in the Far East; and only two of the three required air store issuing ships. The 13 armament store issuing ships needed were, however, all on station by March 1945. The original estimate of five fast replenishment tankers was increased to 14, but even this number was insufficient, as a revised estimate early in 1945 gave a requirement of 18. Out of the 14 tankers on station, however, only four could reach 15 knots ('Wave' class, ex-Empire standard wartime construction equipped with the latest RAS gear); the remaining 10 tankers being the earlier 'Dale' and 'Ranger' classes, which could only just make 11 knots, had antiquated RAS gear, and whose cargo capacity was far too low to be of great value in supplying the needs of the BPF. Fortunately the Americans were very understanding and although the agreed principle was that the BPF should be fully self-supporting, it was able in a number of cases to use the facilities of the American Fleet Train.

After World War II improvements continued to be made with RAS. The jackstay was improved as a means of transferring light loads of up to one ton between ships, and was further adapted as a means for supporting fuel pipe lines between ships; the derricks remaining in their stowed position. This use of the jackstay for abeam refuelling allowed greater separation between vessels, especially important with carriers, which were soon to be fitted with the angled flight deck which gave much greater overhang than hitherto experienced.

With the start of the Korean War in June 1950, the RFA again found itself deficient in certain types of supply vessels, and recourse was again made to the facilities of the American Fleet Train. During the war a further development to RAS underwent experiment on board the victualling store issuing ship *Fort Duquesne*. For the experiment a platform was built over the stern of the supply ship from which a Westland Sikorsky Dragonfly helicopter was used to test the practicability of Vertical Underway Replenishment (VERTREP).

(This as not the first instance of replenishment using a helicopter, however. The first known transfer by helicopter took place in April 1945 when three 'Hoverfly's' of 711 Squadron, based at Hatston, carried underslung loads of up to 60lb from shore to ship.)

The Korean War, the Suez operations of 1956, the Indonesian confrontation, the Beira patrol (see below) and other incidents, together with the withdrawal of the Royal Navy from many of its overseas bases in the late 1960's, has focussed attention on the need for a well balanced RFA, and the necessity for possessing suitable vessels capable of carrying out underway replenishment under all sorts of conditions. The 'Fort' class stores vessels and 'Wave' class tankers are no longer capable of meeting the needs of a nuclear age fleet, and have reached the end of their useful life.

Modern naval forces dictate that RAS should be completed at the utmost speed. Warships so engaged are extremely vulnerable,

being unable to carry out high speed manoeuvres to avoid attacks, which today can be mounted within minutes of detection. The old 'Fort' and 'Wave' classes are not capable of high speed replenishment and cannot carry the wide range of items needed by a modern task force (up to 18,000 different items of varying quantities are required for one 'County' class destroyer as opposed to 2,000 items World War II destroyer). To meet modern requirements converted merchant ships are no longer a practicable proposition.

HMS Fearless refuelling from the replenishment tanker *Tideflow*. The *Tideflow* is one of three vessels built during the 1950's to replace the ageing vessels of the 'Wave' class. *[MoD, RN, Official*

The need for *fast* supply vessels became so urgent during the 1950's, that as an interim measure three newly completed merchant ships were purchased. Named *Resurgent, Retainer* and *Reliant*, these 15 knot cargo vessels underwent extensive modification to enable them to carry out RAS under modern combat conditions. Their refits incorporated many new ideas to speed up the movement of stores, and the holds were equipped with high speed lifts. Special stowage for the multitudinous range of stores has been built into some of the holds, while others have been given environmental control in the form of refrigeration, humidity, and air-conditioning, to keep stores in perfect condition. To dispense the wide range of items carried, transfer points equipped with self-tensioning winches have been provided fore and aft to port and starboard.

Also during the 1950's a new tanker was designed to replace the ageing vessels of the 'Wave' class. Designed from the outset for RAS, the 'Tide' class have profited from previous experience with the 'Wave' class, a number of which have had their RAS equipment modernised to the standards of the early 'Tide' class. The new tankers are much larger than the 'Wave' class (16,800 tons as opposed to 11,950 tons deadweight) and in addition are fitted to carry a limited tonnage of dry cargo. The fuelling rigs are of a new design too, the pole derricks of the 'Wave' class being replaced by a lattice rig all serviced with sophisticated winches, while the fuelling hoses are fitted with self-sealing couplings. There are three fuel replenishment points to port and two to starboard, aft of the bridge, while a single pole mast supports two derricks in the forward well deck. From the forward well deck replenishment of dry cargo stores by jackstay is also carried out.

With the three new tankers of the early 'Tide' class operational (*Tideflow, Tidereach* and *Tidesurge*), attention turned to the design of a new class of supply vessels. With the vast range of items required by modern warships a whole new system of storage and supply has had to be designed. Means have

had to be found for speeding up the movement of supplies from the holds to the replenishment point, as well as improvements to the actual RAS gear. One of the most important points of the design of this new 'Ness' class supply vessels is a covered roadway 328ft long by 38ft wide on No 1 deck. This clearway is served by high speed lifts, one of which is connected to each of the holds. From the lifts, fork lift trucks (another innovation on board supply ships) rapidly transfer stores along the clearway to the requisite replenishment point. Here the trucks deposit their loads onto powered roller conveyers which move the stores to the transfer point. Further simplification and speed up has been achieved by the use of standard sized pallets, which as far as is practicable are pre-packed ashore before being loaded into the supply vessel. Loads unsuitable for palletisation because of their size are handled by nylon cargo nets, slings or crates. In the holds, a number of which are temperature controlled and a number humidity controlled, collapsable storage bins, trays and drawers are used wherever possible for such small items that cannot be practically palletised. These items are then transferred by roller conveyers to points where they can be assembled as required onto the pallets. The design of the storage pens has been made as flexible as possible to give maximum utilisation of hold space, while at the same time giving ample room for access to the 6,000 different items carried. Another innovation used to speed up transfer is the use of closed circuit television which keeps a close watch on all movements in the clearway, while overall control of RAS operations is exercised from a central office sited amidships on the RAS deck. Large watertight doorways give access to each of the six replenishment points from the clearway. Samson posts at each of the replenishment points are so built that loads can now be lifted vertically before beginning their journey across to the receiving vessel on the jackstay. One other notable feature of the 'Ness' class, and one which has now become a regular feature on all newly completed supply vessels, is a helicopter platform sited over the

Storage bins for small articles in the supply ship
Lyness   *[MoD, RN, Official*

Each of the transfer points on the new supply ships
of the 'Ness' class is fed by a powered roller
conveyor.   *[Lansing Bagnall*

The firm of Lansing Bagnall have supplied the
Admiralty with fork lift trucks for use on board the
'Ness' class. The 'Rapide' fork lift truck is capable
of negotiating wet decks with a one ton load and
can continue operations under conditions of 15
degrees of roll or camber of the deck.
                                 [Lansing Bagnall

The engines of the 'Ness' class can be controlled
from an air conditioned space by one man.
                                 [MoD, RN, Official

Lyness, the first of the new supply ships to be completed.

[MoD, RN, Official

poop deck. Served by a high speed lift from the clearway and No 4 hold, this platform provides yet another replenishment point from which VERTREP operations can be carried out. This system enables a warship to continue with its normal duties while at the same time receiving replenishment from the supply vessel.

While the 'Ness' class supply vessels were under design two new replenishment tankers were built. The new '01' class tankers are an improved design of two later vessels of the 'Tide' class—*Tidepool* and *Tidespring*. The '01' class are capable of issuing five different types of fuel simultaneously, as well as fresh water. In addition drummed oil products can be transferred from a helicopter platform aft. Among the new techniques used to simplify RAS operations, and to reduce the number of crew required to man the vessels, is a data logging and alarm scanning system. This new equipment makes it possible to monitor all machinery operations thus enabling faults to be traced in the shortest possible time. Further monitors give remote readings of the amount of fuel remaining in the tanks while tank and hose valves can all be remotely controlled from a central office at the rear of the bridge, which commands a full view of the RAS deck. Speed has been improved in the new tankers and the specially strengthened hull enables them to operate with reasonable safety in the icy wastes of the Arctic.

For small escort forces and convoy work a smaller class of tankers—the 'Rover' class—has been designed. These vessels too are equipped to replenish warships whilst under way with fuel, fresh water, limited dry stores and refrigerated cargo under all sorts of weather conditions.

Following the feasibility studies, which led to the design of the 'Ness' class, further plans were drawn up for another new class of supply ships. Although designed primarily as ammunition replenishment vessels for supplying the SEASLUG, SEACAT, SEA DART missiles etc., the *Regent* and *Resource* also carry a wide range of victualling and naval stores. The replenishment equipment of these armament vessels is similar to that on board the 'Ness' class, and includes high speed lifts for the transfer of cargo from the holds to the RAS deck.

When in 1906 the first experiments in RAS

A helicopter platform is built over the stern of the 'Ness' class, and from here VERTREP operations are carried out.　　[MoD, RN, Official

were carried out it was little thought that one day the Royal Navy would be almost wholly dependant on this service for its supplies. In those days RAS was only used to back up the facilities obtained at the many shore bases overseas. During World War I RAS techniques were not sufficiently advanced enough for them to be relied upon with certainty and after World War I money was insufficient for the RFA to expand or to carry out many experiments.

In the meantime the aircraft carrier and submarine had revolutionised naval warfare. It was at last realised that useful though static bases overseas might be, their usefulness remained only so long as Great Britain exercised full power over them, both politically and militarily. Those bases over which we could only expect to maintain a tenuous hold, might well lose their viability in the face of air attack. Before the RFA could carry out plans for expansion, however, World War II began. The gloomy predictions of 1936 soon became all too true, and the Royal Navy was denied any kind of base facility in Europe from the coast of Norway right round to Gibraltar. In the Mediterranean the nearness of Italian aerodromes made Malta untenable for a time, and for many months the only safe bases were at Gibraltar and Alexandria, but even these were subject to attacks by daring frogmen. In the Far East the Japanese captured many bases and made others untenable. Provided Great Britain had had sufficient

The new replenishment tanker *Olna* carrying out RAS operations with *HMS London* and *HMS Argonaut*

[MoD, RN, Official

The helicopter platform built out over the stern of the replenishment tanker *Olna*. Note the roller near the stern. From here fuel hoses are paid out for astern refuelling.   [*A. J. Watts collection*

The small replenishment tanker *Green Rover*.
[*MoD, RN, Official*

warships available and if we had had an adequate replenishment group in the Indian Ocean, it would have been possible for the Royal Navy to remain in eastern waters in strength.

Nearer home the disadvantage of the short radius of action of the escorts became all too apparent during convoy operations. Admiral Horton pointed out in 1942 that 'only vessels of long fuel endurance are of any use for escorting ocean trade convoys.' At that time escorts were unable to cross the Atlantic and carry out anti-submarine operations as well. The escorts at that time worked on a series of relays, leaving convoys to refuel at Iceland or Newfoundland. Not until the Spring of 1943, when it became general practice to sail supply tankers with the convoys, was the problem overcome.

In the 1963 Defence Estimates it was stated that 'In order to ensure that Naval resources are deployed to the best advantage everywhere, it is essential to economise, wherever possible, in shore support'. With the almost complete withdrawal of the Royal Navy from overseases bases, and its concentration in home waters, is there now the same need for a large modern fleet of replenishment vessels? At first it might seem that the answer to this question is no. Nothing could be further from the truth! The Royal Navy today is more dependant than ever upon RAS facilities to carry out its role of protecting the free trade of Great Britain. If that trade, practically all of which is carried in merchant ships, is threatened, then the crews of the merchant ships look to the Royal Navy for support; either moral or material. The Royal Navy is also one of the instruments of British policy and just one example will serve to show the dependance of the Navy upon RAS in these circumstances. Ever since Rhodesia proclaimed the Unilateral Declaration of Independence units of the Royal Navy have been employed in carrying out a blockade off Mozambique. All vessels heading for ports in that country have been closely watched to see if they are carrying goods banned to the Smith regime by the United Nations. The vessels of the Royal Navy

Armament supply vessel *Regent*.

employed on the Beira patrol have been able to maintain their blockade only because of the RAS facilities provided by the RFA.

Having examined the need for a fleet of modern replenishment vessels the next question is "Do we have sufficient vessels of the right type?" At the present time the RFA would seem to be well equipped with modern vessels, such as described above, sufficient to meet the needs of the Navy today. But we must always look to the future. Already a new generation of warships is under design, and it is planned that these new vessels should be capable of spending far longer periods at sea, being able to operate with fewer refits and self-maintenance periods. This in turn will

place a greater strain on the supply services, requiring larger quantities of stores to be available on the spot. In this context is a modern force of three stores vessels, four ammunition ships (two design built and two converted merchant ships) and eight tankers sufficient? The answer would seem to be no, for the £70 million building programme announced on November 11th, 1971, included two fleet replenishment ships of a new design. Even supply ships need restocking and with their highly sophisticated systems of storekeeping and stock-piling it is difficult for them to replenish at sea from cargo ships, and they would probably find it necessary to return to Great Britain to restock. If this is the

RFA Tidesurge refuels the carrier *Ark Royal* and frigate *Troubridge* on patrol in the Beira Straits in 1966.

Fleet supply tanker *Derwentdale* refuelling a commando carrier. Although normally only employed on freighting duties, these super tankers of the 'Dale' class can also carry out RAS using the astern method of refuelling.

[MoD, RN, Official

case then to support a naval force in a distant ocean *at least* three supply vessels are necessary; one to be on station, with one each returning from and proceeding to the replenishment group. So it would seem, that for any protracted emergency, the RFA is operating with the minimum number of *up to date* replenishment vessels. The tanker situation is not so critical, for the RFA operates a small number of large freighting tankers which are fully capable of topping up the replenishment tankers and in some cases providing RAS facilities as well. It is in the

victualling, naval store, and especially ammunition and missile spheres that supply vessels are in the greatest demand and ships such as the *Regent* and *Resource* which can supply both naval stores, and a limited quantity of victuals as well as missiles, are the most satisfactory type of replenishment vessel.

At long last, after many years of being regarded as the Cinderella of the Senior Service, the RFA is being accorded the attention which should be attached to its functions, and for the present, at least, the situation in regard to RAS, is well in hand.

The Royal Navy
at Sea

ANTHONY J. WATTS

An anti-submarine helicopter observer plotting a position.

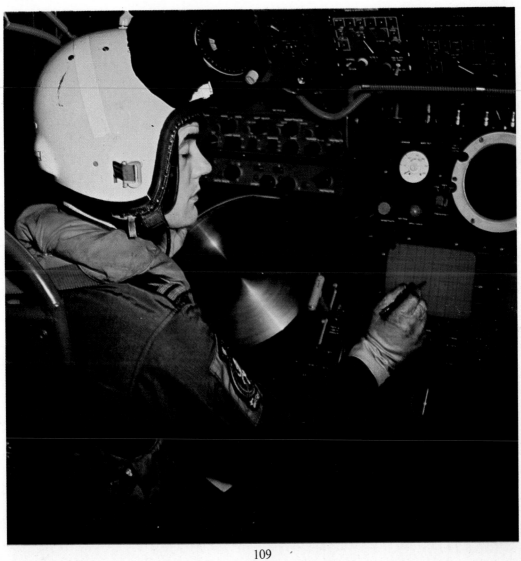

RFA Tarbatness transferring stores in the South China Sea.

Ships' divers.

HMS Blake firing a 'Seacat' guided missile.

Loading a 'Seacat' guided missile on to a launcher aboard *HMS London*.

'Limbo' anti-submarine mortars being prepared for a shoot on a Leander class frigate.

A Wasp helicopter landing on the flight deck of *HMS Aurora*.

Vosper Thornycroft Frigates

ANTHONY J. WATTS

When the two south of England shipbuilding firms of Vosper and John I. Thornycroft amalgamated in 1966, they combined one of the finest design teams in the world with a firm whose reputation for fast patrol boat construction was second to none. Previous to the amalgamation, Thornycroft's had specialised in the design and construction of frigates and destroyers. Since the amalgamation the firm has specialised in designing warships in the fast patrol boat and frigate categories. These craft have been designed with the export market in mind, especially the emergent and small nations wishing to modernise, or build from scratch, new navies. With this in mind the resulting designs have tended towards the less sophisticated type of vessel, capable of being run and maintained by smaller nations. In addition to being less complicated than vessels built for the Royal Navy, they have, as a result of this simplification, been cheaper to construct, a vital factor when selling such craft to small nations with only very limited defence budgets.

The frigates designed by the Vosper Thornycroft group have all been based upon the 'Leander' class vessels of the Royal Navy. Taking this class as the basis, Vosper Thornycroft have developed a frigate which is only half the size of the 'Leander' class, and at about half the cost. The initial planning led to the design of the Mark V frigate. One of the most important features of this design is the interchangeability of the armament, that fitted being very much the customers choice to suit

The first frigate to be designed by the Vosper Thornycroft group was the Mark V. Having gained experience with the corvette *Tobruk* built for the Libyan Navy and taking the design of the Royal Navy's "Leander" class frigates as a basis, Vosper's developed the Mark V. So successful was the design that four of these vessels have been ordered by the Iranian Navy. The first of the four Mark V's to be completed was the *Saam.* They are extremely good looking vessels with excellent lines. Although designed to mount the new 4.5-inch Mark 8, these vessels at the present carry an older Mark of 4.5-inch.

[Vosper Thornycroft Group

The Mark V design has been uprated into the Mark VII, the extra displacement allowing the vessels to carry rather more powerful armament and more equipment. With larger bunkers the radius of action has also been increased. The increase in displacement, however, has been at the expense of speed. One of these vessels is at present under construction for the Libyan Navy.

[Vosper Thornycroft Group

The Mark VII design is now being developed into the even larger Mark X, six of which have been ordered by the Brazilian Navy. All the vessels are very similar in appearance.　*[Vosper Thornycroft Group*

A slightly different design has been produced for the Royal Navy's Type 21 frigate. Using the same parameters laid down for the earlier designs, Vosper Thornycroft have produced an extremely practical design, which like their other frigates, has kept complements to a reasonable level—about 170 in the case of the Type 21. Again the overall appearance of the Type 21 is very similar to the other frigates designed by Vosper Thornycroft.

[Vosper Thornycroft Group

his own requirements. The basic design remains the same for all vessels. The only disadvantage, if it can be called such, is that the resulting vessel does not have an all round capability. On the other hand, being that much cheaper than a larger vessel, a smaller navy could in all probability acquire two or three such vessels, with a variety of different armaments and combine the vessels into a powerful general purpose group. Now the advantage can be plainly seen, for with a standard design, maintenance and spare part availability is greatly simplified and costs kept to a minimum. Apart from the above factors the designers have also allowed space in the design for the installation of extra equipment, a development factor which applies to all warships in these days of rapid technological advancement.

The initial Mark V frigate design was developed into the Mark VII, a vessel slightly larger than the Mark V, but with the same propulsion unit. Being larger, the Mark VII is able to mount a heavier armament than the Mark V, and with a larger radius of action is capable of rather more sustained operations

than the earlier design. The only disadvantage of the Mark VII is that the cruising and maximum speed are lower than the Mark V, resulting from the increased tonnage. Both designs use diesel engines for cruising while gas turbines can provide short concentrated bursts of high speeds of up to 39 knots ($37\frac{1}{2}$ knots in the Mark VII).

The mark VII frigate design is now being developed into the Mark X, six of which have been ordered for the Brazilian Navy. Like the earlier frigate designs, the Mark X is exceptionally economical in its complement, a reduction of fifty per cent being attained over other comparable vessels. The reduction in complement has been achieved by allowing for a greater degree of base maintenance, and a minimum of onboard maintenance. As with the earlier designs cost reduction has also been achieved by complete lack of armour protection, and the ignoring of the underwater noise factor. These designs rely on speed and manoeuvrability for their self-defence. The Mark X design has more than doubled in size over the earlier Mark VII, while maximum and cruising speeds are much reduced (30 and

The high speed propulsion unit in all the Vosper Thornycroft frigates is the Rolls-Royce Olympus gas turbine, a model of which is shown here. This unit has been designed especially for marine use to provide high revolutions instantaneously, and without the machinery taking up a great deal of valuable space in the hull of the warship.

[Rolls-Royce

22 knots as designed). On the other hand the much larger tonnage allows the vessels to mount a more powerful armament than the earlier designs: viz:

Mk V: One 4.5in Mk 8 and either a 40mm Bofors or a SEACAT launcher; a helicopter landing pad or a surface-to-surface missile launcher; a Limbo A/S mortar and either another SEACAT launcher or a twin 35mm Oerlikon.

Mk VII: Two 4.5in Mk 8, a Bofors A/S rocket launcher, a 40mm and a twin 35mm or one 4.5in, two SEACAT launchers, two 40mm and an A/S helicopter.

Mk X: GP design: two 4.5in Mk 8, 40mm Bofors, EXOCET surface-to-surface missile launchers, SEACAT surface-to-air missile launchers, one A/S helicopter. A/S design: one 4.5in, IKARA A/S missile launcher, SEACAT surface-to-air missile launcher, one A/S helicopter.

The appearance of the Mk X as depicted by artists is very similar to the previous designs.

In addition to the above, Vosper Thornycroft have also designed, at the request of the Admiralty, the Type 21 frigate for the Royal Navy. In appearance this design is very similar to the other frigate designs. The Type 21 differs from the earlier designs, however, in having the COGOG (COmbined Gas turbine Or Gas turbine) arrangement instead of the CODOG (COmbined Diesel Or Gas turbine). As with the other frigate designs the Rolls Royce Olympus gas turbine has been used for high speeds while for cruising the vessels are equipped with the Rolls Royce Tyne gas turbine. The Type 21 frigate is the first vessel to be designed and constructed for all gas turbine propulsion. The armament planned for the Type 21 is as follows, but like the earlier designs this can be adjusted to suit the customers requirements:

One 4.5in Mk 8, two 20mm, one quadruple SEACAT launcher (to be replaced later by the more powerful SEAWOLF), six torpedo tubes and one A/S helicopter.

Ship-Borne Helicopters

DAVID J. BROWN

On September 9th, 1936, a Royal Air Force Cierva C.30A Rota landed on the Royal Navy's aircraft carrier *Furious*. Trials were undertaken from the ship while she lay at anchor, and while she steamed in the Channel. The C.30A was an autogiro—a STOL (Short Take-Off and Landing) rather than a VTOL (Vertical Take-Off and Landing) aircraft— but this was, nevertheless, the first evaluation of a rotary-wing aircraft as a naval weapon, and the limitations of the small autogiro applied to small helicopters until the early 1960's.

Interest in the C.30A as a naval aircraft had stemmed from a wish to extend the capability for air operations to ships too small or unsuited for the operation of seaplanes. The value of aircraft for reconnaissance, anti-submarine patrols, and for spotting for the guns of the Fleet was only too obvious, and the STOL or VTOL aircraft possessed (and possesses) certain advantages over 'conventional' aircraft, with their need for a clear area for the take-off and landing runs. Aircraft carriers were operating wheeled aircraft, and many cruisers and battleships were equipped with catapults and cranes for seaplanes, but the former were expensive ships, and available only in small numbers, and the latter suffered many disadvantages from their 'aviation arrangements'—catapults and hangers were space-consuming, the ship had to slow down, or even stop, to recover the aircraft. A rotary-wing aircraft could be operated from a small open space, or a platform over a gun mounting or a deck-house, on a merchant ship as well as on an auxiliary or a small warship.

Unfortunately, the C.30A lacked the power and load-lifting capacity to carry two aircrew, the necessary Wireless Telegraphy (W/T) set, navigation equipment, and even a dinghy, let alone a weapon, without sacrificing fuel. As its endurance was less than two hours to start with, it could hardly begin to meet the Royal Navy's requirements.

The first practical helicopters to be considered for naval application were of United States and German origin. In 1938, the Kriegsmarine ordered half-a-dozen Flettner Fl.265 single-seat helicopters for evaluation in the reconnaissance and patrol roles from ship platforms. By 1940, the idea had been sufficiently developed, and trials had indicated the promise of the helicopter, so that a more developed design, the Fl.282, was ordered. The Fl.282 'Kolibri' was a two seater with a 150hp piston-engine, an endurance of less than an hour, and a safe radius of action of about 30 miles—without a weapon load. As a single-seater, it could either carry a minimal weapon load—a 60kg (132lb) bomb—or fuel for two hours. In 1943 and 1944 a number of Fl.282s were used operationally from warship platforms in the Baltic, flying anti-submarine patrols and mine-spotting sorties. As an evaluation, the programme was successful, but the limited excess of power over that required for lift meant that the helicopter was not a viable weapon without further development.

On the other side of the Atlantic, the United States Navy and Coastguard had evinced early interest in Igor Sikorsky's VS-300. This aircraft was the pattern for the majority of Western helicopter designers in the 32 years which have passed since it made its first untethered flight in May 1940. With an anti-torque tail rotor and an efficient directional control system, it opened the way for the development of more powerful rotor-craft. The first of these was the Sikorsky R-4: flying for the first time in January 1942, it was a two-seater with a fully-enclosed cabin and, in its R-4B form, a 180hp engine. It was lighter and carried more fuel than its German contemporary, but it still lacked the load-

Kamov Ka-26 'Hormone' ASW helicopter aboard
the Soviet Navy helicopter carrier *Moskva*. Note
flotation 'boots' around undercarriage wheels.

[via A. J. Watts

carrying capacity required by the United
States and Royal Navies, the latter receiving
a number under Lend-Lease terms. In January
1943, two Royal Navy Hoverflies commenced
trials aboard the merchant ship *Daghestan*,
undertaking at least one convoy operation.
Again, the idea was confirmed as good, but
performance fell short of satisfactory—the
Hoverfly could carry either a depth-charge or
an Observer: in the North Atlantic a navigator
was essential if radio and radar aids were not
available. In any case, by the time that the
R-4B was ready for such operations, the
Allies had just sufficient escort carriers and

Merchant Aircraft Carriers to accompany or
provide close support for most important
convoys.

In the American Army Air Force service,
the R-4B was used for communications and
casualty evacuation during the latter part of
the War, and it was in these roles that naval
helicopters saw most of their service until the
early 1950's. From 1949, the US Navy
embarked Sikorsky HO2S S-51s in aircraft
carriers as communications and rescue—
'planeguard'—aircraft, and the Royal Navy
followed suit in 1951, using the same aircraft
as modified by Westland aircraft—the

118

Dragonfly. Off Korea, the aircraft were used from time to time for mine-spotting, but this was the limit of their warlike potential.

During the late 1940's, the navies of the United States, Britain and the Soviet Union all conducted experiments with helicopters operating from platforms on small warships. In 1947, the 'River' class frigate *Helmsdale* was fitted with a small flight deck aft, and an R-4B undertook trials over a period of some months. The lack of a suitable helicopter, with small dimensions and power to spare, prevented the Royal Navy from taking advantage of the experience until the early 1950's, and then not in a front-line role.

The Soviet Navy, lacking aircraft-carrying ships, and at this time, overseas bases for land-based maritime air support, was also drawn to the possibilities of the helicopter. In 1949, a small batch of Kamov Ka-10 (NATO codename—Hat) 55hp piston-engined helicopters was procured for evaluation, operating from platforms on light cruisers, ice-breakers, and survey ships in an extensive series of trials which lasted for some three years. These aircraft were very much 'first-generation' models, and the Ka-15 Hen which followed in 1952, with an in-service date of 1955, was little more advanced, apart from its control system. With a 255hp radial engine, the Ka-15 had a disposable load of about 750lbs (340kg) at normal take-off weight—with the normal allowance of 200lbs (91kg) per member of aircrew, this left only 350lbs (160kg) for fuel and weapons, with a fuel consumption of approximately 150lbs (70kg) per hour in cruising, as opposed to hovering flight. The Ka-15 appeared at the 1955 Tushino Air Display carrying a pair of dummy missiles and a small 'chin'-mounted radome, thereby persuading the Western aviation Press that it was in service as a viable shipborne weapon. Although the Ka-15 was subsequently embarked in Soviet warships and fishing fleet factory ships, its capability as a weapon was extremely limited and the main benefit gained must have been from the experience.

The American Navy and Coastguard,

supported by the quickly expanding American helicopter industry, investigated several aspects of shipborne helicopter utilisation. Personnel transfer and rescue were the first roles for which the aircraft were embarked, aboard battleships of the 'Iowa' class and heavy cruisers of the 'Baltimore' class; these ships already had hangars below the quarter-deck, with a capacity of between three and four floatplanes, and the modifications required were minimal, consisting of the removal of the catapults and the application of a non-skid landing area right aft. From 1950, Piasecki HUP (UH-25) utility helicopters were embarked in these ships, replacing the Sikorsky HO2S.

The American Coast Guard Cutter *Edisto* was fitted with a small flight deck in 1948, and a Bell HTL (H-13) light helicopter embarked for general observation, liaison, and rescue duties. *Edisto* was an ice-breaker, as were her sister ships—later also fitted with flight decks —and the aircraft was found to be extremely useful for searching for clear water and passages through pack ice. In 1949, the Royal Canadian Navy ordered an Arctic Patrol Vessel of similar design, incorporating a flight deck. When HMCS *Labrador* first appeared in 1954, she had no hangar, but after a few months experience, a prefabricated structure was added and accommodation provided for two Sikorsky S-55s (US Navy HO4S). In the same year, the USS *Glacier*—a follow-on design to the *Edisto*—appeared; she was noteworthy in that she was the first United States Navy unit to feature a hangar for her helicopters in the original design.

So far, the regular service parent ships had been relatively large. The cutter types were beamy vessels, designed for good sea-keeping qualities which provided a stable landing platform and parking area. In 1949, the Royal Navy ordered a survey ship with an integral hangar and flight deck. HMS *Vidal* had a beam of only 40 feet, and her standard tonnage was only 1,565 tons—less than a third of that of the *Labrador*: helicopters were going to operate from really small ships at last. The *Vidal* entered service in 1954, with a

Fairey Ultra-Light Helicopter during trials aboard *HMS Grenville*. The flight deck party in the port-side nets have light lines attached to the quick release clips securing the aircraft (which carries the civil registration G-APJJ, in spite of its roundel and 'Royal Navy' blazon)   *[via Author*

Westland Dragonfly (S-51) for general com-munications, photographic survey, and stores transfers.

Between 1950 and 1960, there were many other such non-combat helicopter deploy-ments to ships fitted with flight decks, and in some cases with hangars. The United Whalers factory ship *Balaena* carried a pair of S-51s with her to the Antarctic for whale-spotting during the 1950/51 season.

Although the lack of a small helicopter with a good fuel/warload combination prevented the serious application of the aircraft as a small ship weapon, great advances were being made in the utilisation of medium helicopters as Anti-Submarine Warfare (ASW) weapons. Although several designers contributed, Si-korsky Aircraft emerged as the clear leaders in this field, the HO4S-3 entering service with the American Navy in 1951, succeeded from August 1955 by the HSS-1, and in September 1961 the HSS-2 (subsequently re-designated and up-dated as the SH-3D) joined the Fleet. All three designs were used by other Navies, built not only by Sikorsky, but also by British, French, Japanese, and Italian firms. Westland Aircraft are the only company to have built all three aircraft, modified to suit British requirements, as the Whirlwind, Wessex, and Sea King.

The medium helicopters carry a sonar system similar to that fitted to surface ships, but with the added advantage that the sensor head—the transducer—can be lowered to greater depths than those possible with a hull-mounted ship sonar, thus searching below the layers of water of differing temperature which diffuse, refract, and reflect the high-power sound pulses. The HO4S/Whirlwind could carry either the sonar or a weapon load, but the later aircraft, both of which are still in front-line service with several Navies, can

carry both simultaneously, to enable the aircraft to follow up its own contacts unsupported if need be.

Four other helicopter designs have been employed as medium ASW aircraft. A small number of Vertol Model 44As were supplied to the Swedish Navy in 1958–59 for inshore anti-submarine operations from land bases; known as the HKP-1, these aircraft were fitted with sonar. In Russia, the Mil Mi-4 Hound entered Soviet Navy service, equipped with a radar and a 'towed-bird' Magnetic Anomaly Detector (MAD), also for shore-based operations. As MAD is a short-range sensor, intended to be used as a method of fixing the exact position of a submarine by measuring the deviations in the earth's magnetic field below the equipment, the Hound's initial detection capability against a submerged submarine was probably negligible, and it was used in conjunction with surface ships or with aircraft using sonobuoys.

In July 1961, the Kamov Ka-25 helicopter was displayed at Tushino, carrying a radar and two small air-to-surface missiles on outriggers on the fuselage sides. Initially given the NATO codename Harp, this aircraft was further developed and by 1968, when it appeared aboard the helicopter carrier *Moskva*, it had been re-named Hormone. With approximately the same payload and all-up weight as the Sikorsky S-58 derivatives (HSS-1, SH-34J, Wessex), the Hormone is equipped with radar, MAD, and, it is believed, sonobuoys. Some aircraft have been seen with a small fairing under the empennage which might be a radar receiver for passive electronic countermeasures. The Hormone is appreciably smaller than the S-58, for with the Kamov system of contra-rotating main rotors on a single mast, no tail pylon and anti-torque rotor are needed, although a small aircraft-type empennage is retained for stability in forward flight. The Hormone's main employment appears to have been aboard the two large helicopter carriers *Moskura* and *Leningrad*, but the guided-missile cruisers of the 'Kresta' class have a flight deck and hangar capable of operating

the type, presumably as part of the surface-to-surface missile system, rather than as an ASW weapon.

The fourth non-American medium helicopter is the French Sud Aviation SA-321G Super Frelon, a three-engined aircraft which dwarfs the SH-3D Sea King. The Super Frelon entered service with the Aeronavale in 1966, but its size makes it suitable for operation from aircraft carriers and from the helicopter carrier *Jeanne d'Arc*.

All the medium helicopters which embarked for ASW duties prior to 1962 did so aboard aircraft carriers of the United States, Royal, Royal Canadian, Royal Netherlands and French Navies. In the past decade, these-have been joined by the Royal Australian, Brazilian, Argentinian, Italian, Soviet, and Spanish Navies. The Italian and Soviet Navies differ in that all their helicopter carriers are composite ships, with flight and hangar decks aft, while retaining gun and missile armaments forward.

The latest medium helicopter version to enter service is virtually a flying frigate. The SH-3H Sea King has sonar and radar of the latest type, and in addition it carries MAD, sonobuoys, electronic countermeasures equipment, a 'window' dispenser, and a data link receiver, to enable the crew to be provided with tactical information from the ASW defence computer in the parent ship, the computer deriving its information from all sensors in accompanying ships, aircraft, and submarines.

By 1955, the major contributors to the NATO ASW Fleet—Britain, Canada, the United States, the Nertherlands, France, and Italy—had already decided upon the outlines of their carrier-borne helicopter search/attack forces. Provided that carrier support was available for ASW operations, long-range detection and effective attacks with homing torpedoes would be available at ranges outside those of submarine torpedoes. Unsupported, the escorts would be at a serious disadvantage, for their mortars and rocket projectors had a maximum range of about 2000 yards. Greater ranges were possible, but

Sud Aviation (now SNIAS) Alouette 3 lands on
La Galissoniere. The gratings on the narrow deck
are to receive the harpoon used to secure the
helicopter immediately prior to touch-down:
the point of the harpoon can be discerned between
the main undercarriage wheels.

[ECA via M. H Le Masson

with longer time in flight, miss distances were
bound to increase, particularly when the
target was a fast submarine with good
manoeuvrability. Some form of mid-course
guidance was necessary if a homing torpedo
was to enter the water within acquisition
range of its target.

Two solutions were adopted. The United
States, French, and Royal Australian Navies
opted for a remotely-controlled unmanned
'drone' weapon delivery vehicle—ASROC,
MALAFON, and IKARA—carrying a single homing torpedo out to ranges in excess of five
miles. Guidance was provided by the launching ship, depending upon information from
the ship's sonar. The long detection ranges
would be available when Variable Depth
Sonar (VDS) gear was fitted, able to lower
the sonar transducer below the layers, after
the fashion of helicopter sonars.

The Royal, Royal Canadian, Royal Netherlands, and Italian Navies preferred to develop
a light helicopter as a weapons carrier. A
manned system, depending upon radio or

data link direction, could be launched and controlled even if the parent ship was not in contact, giving much greater flexibility and almost infinite re-usability, not only as an ASW weapon, but also as a general utility aircraft and, possibly, as a surface reconnaissance and strike aircraft. A very important peace-time consideration was that training can be continuous and tactics can be up-dated with a helicopter, whereas the drone system is restricted to a very limited number of 'live' firings, due to the cost of each round, and most exercises must end with a dummy run, making evaluation an academic exercise.

The most important single engineering development which made the light helicopter a practical ASW proposition was the production of the small turbine engine, which provided more power per unit of engine weight than any piston engine of similar rating. The weight thus 'saved' could be used for additional fuel or payload while keeping the overall weight of the helicopter down. Not until the early 1960's were the operational light helicopters to enter service, after a lengthy development and evaluation process; in the meantime, a number of medium helicopter/small ship combinations appeared.

In early 1957, the Royal Canadian Navy 'River' class frigate *Buckingham* was fitted with a platform over her quarterdeck, and a Sikorsky HO4S-3 was embarked for trials as an ASW search/strike weapon. The trials were successful and in August 1957 the deck was dismantled and re-erected on the modern 'St. Laurent' class frigate *Ottawa*, the evaluation continuing to the end of the year. Armed with this experience, the Canadians began preparatory work on the design of a new class of DDHs—helicopter-carrying destroyers, and the re-design of the seven 'St Laurent' class vessels. As the Canadian Navy had only one aircraft carrier—the *Bonaventure*—the DDHs' flights would be equipped with a combined search/strike aircraft, to provide an air ASW capability when detached from the carrier, and also to cover the periods when the carrier would be "off the line" for refit.

The choice of aircraft was ambitious. The CHSS-3D Sea King was selected—an aircraft with a rotors-turning length of some 80ft and an all-up-weight of nearly ten tons. Even when folded for stowage, the Sea King is 54ft 9in long, with a span over the undercarriage sponsons of 20ft. Deck landings in rough weather, with the main wheels only a couple of yards from the deck edges would be 'interesting' at the best of times, and handling such a heavy aircraft on the flight deck of a ship of destroyer size would be sufficiently difficult in calm weather, let alone in the Atlantic winter.

Most of the problems were overcome at a stroke, with the design of the 'Bear Trap' haul-down system. By securing a cable from the helicopter to a fish-plate in the centre of the deck, the Sea King could winch itself down the last 20ft, the pilot judging the exact moment of touch-down. Once down, the aircraft would be folded (main rotors and tail pylon) and the fish-plate would then be moved up a slot in the deck, towing the Sea King until it was fully stowed in the hangar.

The first Canadian DDH, *Assiniboine*, commissioned after conversion, in June 1963. From being a conventional frigate, she had been transformed into a rather unconventional helicopter carrier, with two narrow uptakes on either side of the large hangar amidships. The flight deck was approximately at two-thirds of the ship's length from the bows, in order to reduce the effects of the ship's movement to the minimum—a concession made in very few classes of helicopter-carrying escort. The DDH/CHSS-3D combination has been extremely successful, and the concept has been adopted by the American Navy, which will arm its 'Spruance' class large destroyers with a single Sea King apiece.

It has been preceded by a rather more modest approach by the Royal Navy. In 1957, the first of the 'County' class Guided Missile Destroyers was ordered. With a large Surface-to-Air missile launcher right aft, and much of the internal space taken up by magazines and the electronics, no provision could be made for a ship-mounted ASW weapon, such as a mortar, and so a flight deck and

HMS Devonshire, with her Westland Wessex HAS1 about to touch down. The aircraft hangar is forward of the director, necessitating a complicated negotiation of the narrow space on port side. *[MoD(N)]*

hangar were incorporated in the design, for the operation of a Wessex as a weapons carrier, under the direction of the ship, and as a search 'consort' to the ship, using the helicopter's sonar. The first of the eight 'County' class was completed in 1961 and the last in 1970. The Wessex HAS1 has been replaced by the HAS3 in most ships' flights, the later aircraft being fitted with radar and a very efficient sonar, but it is unlikely that the Sea King could be operated without very extensive modification to the ships.

The large 'County' class were expensive ships, and their primary role was not ASW. The Royal Navy wished to provide *all* its modern (post-1960) escorts with helicopters, to be used as weapons carriers. The sonar-fitted Wessex was too sophisticated for this role, and a smaller utility helicopter was required. In 1957, the Fairey Ultra-Light helicopter undertook trials aboard the frigate HMS *Grenville* and the Royal Navy established for itself the advantages and shortcomings of small helicopter operations from a small ship. The development of the small turbine engine as a propulsion unit for helicopters had only recently made the use of light aircraft a practical proposition. The Fairey Ultra-Light was not suitable for development, but in 1958 the Saunder-Roe company brought out the

P.531—a compact light helicopter with obvious development potential. The original parent company was acquired by Westland Aircraft in 1959, and after service trials with the P531-2 in 1960, a development contract was placed for what was to become the Westland Wasp HAS1.

The first Wasp did not fly until October 1962, but production was rapid, and by the end of February 1963, 200 deck landings had been carried out during acceptance trials aboard the 'Tribal' class frigate *Nubian*. The 'Tribal' class have been built with a hangar and superimposed flight deck, part of the latter serving as a lift between the two decks. Seven units were completed between 1961 and 1964 and have seen extensive service, particularly in the Far East and Arabian Gulf. From 1963, the 'Leander' class began to join the Fleet, followed in 1968 by the first of the reconstructed 'Rothesay' class frigates—all with a flight deck aft and a hangar on the same level. The Royal Navy has thus over 30 general-purpose frigates equipped to carry a Wasp. In addition, three 'Hydra' class survey vessels each carry a single Wasp for utility duties; until she was taken out of service in 1971, HMS *Vidal* also carried an aircraft of this type.

Because it was designed specifically for

The flexibility of the light **ASW** helicopter concept—the arrival of **ASROC** or **IKARA** on a sister-ship might be a disaster, but *HMS Euryalus*' Wasp can operate equally efficiently from *HMS Ajax*'s flight deck. The inward 'toeing' of the helicopter's undercarriage wheels can clearly be seen. *[MoD(N)]*

The prototype Westland Lynx. With a three-member wheel undercarriage and internal re-arrangement, this aircraft will replace the Royal Navy's Wasp in the mid-1970's. The Aerospatiale-built Lynxes will embark in the French Navy's helicopter-carrying ASW destroyers.   *[Westland Aircraft*

operation from small ships, the Wasp has been an extremely successful aircraft. No device such as the 'Bear-Trap' is employed for deck landing and handling, but the Wasp's undercarriage and main rotor control system have been adapted to give positive contact with the deck after landing. The forward undercarriage wheels are toed-in 45° and the aft pair toed-out 45°, so that there is little possibility of the aircraft rolling fore or aft after touch-down, and the ability of the pilot to reverse the pitch of the main rotor gives a positive thrust downwards, to hold the aircraft until a nylon lanyard can be secured to the aircraft to hold it down. For handling on the ground (and for landing an airfields) the wheels can be unlocked to castor normally.

The Wasp can carry two Mark 44 anti-submarine torpedoes, or a pair of Mark 11 depth-charges, for release either visually against a periscope or a marker laid on the sea, or under close radar control, against a position established by ship or helicopter sonar. The aircraft carries no sensors, athough a lightweight MAD could probably be carried at the expense of part of the warload. An alternative role for the Wasp is that of an anti-surface ship strike aircraft, for which a pair of AS12 wire-guided missiles are carried on booms on either side of the fuselage. With seating for five passengers it can be, and has been, used for small-scale Commando assault duties.

The Wasp is also in service with the Navies of New Zealand, the Netherlands, and South Africa, and will be sold to India for the 'Leander' class frigates under construction in that country. The Brazilian Navy also uses Wasps, but these are not employed from small ships.

The Royal Navy ordered a replacement for the Wasp in late 1966, the Westland Aircraft and the French Aerospatiale concern commenced design work on the WG.13, a utility and ASW aircraft to replace the Wasp and Scout in the Royal Navy and Army, and the Alouette in French service. The first WG.13, now named Lynx, flew in March 1971 and it is expected that it will be in service with the Royal Navy in 1973. A larger aircraft than the Wasp, with an overall length of nearly 50 ft compared with the 40 ft of the Wasp, the Lynx will employ a 'harpoon' securing system, controlled entirely from the aircraft to provide exact centring above the flight deck. The weapons load will be the same as that of the Wasp, but a lightweight radar will be installed and sufficient 'spare' weight is available for the fitting of MAD, or even sonar (at the expense of weapons).

The United States Navy did not entirely abandon the idea of a ship-borne helicopter as a long-range ASW weapons delivery vehicle, but the emphasis remained on the vehicular system. In December 1958, a contract was signed with the Gyrodyne company for the development of a drone helicopter, to be remotely controlled from its parent ship. The QH-50C flew in the spring of 1961, but two years elapsed before ship acceptance trials were successfully completed, aboard the 'Sumner' class destroyer *Buck*. The American Navy's new escort programme included over 60 ships fitted to operate the Drone Anti-Submarine Helicopter (DASH), and the older destroyers modified to the standards of the Fleet Rehabilitation and Modernisation, Stage 2, programme (FRAM II) were also fitted for, but not in all cases with, DASH. By the end of 1966 over 100 ships were equipped with the QH-50D drone, capable of carrying a pair of Mk 44 torpedoes out to 50 miles. The programme was not entirely successful. Quite apart from any operational shortcomings—manned helicopters and fixed-wing aircraft displayed a marked reluctance to remain in the same area with a QH-50D—the drone was unusable in any utility role, and even its combat application was limited to ASW.

In 1970, the United States Navy publicised its requirements for a Light Airborne Multi-Purpose System to replace DASH as the escort-borne helicopter. Not only was the aircraft to have an ASW and surface strike capability, but it was to be able to carry and fire the SPARROW air-to-air missile, for use against the STYX cruise surface-to-surface missile fired by the 'Osa' and 'Komar' classes of Fast Patrol Boat in service with many Communist and 'non-aligned' Navies. Other equipment was to include radar, MAD, sonobuoys to be monitored by surface ships, and a data link, to pass target information from ship and helicopter sensors through a tactical computer.

The main contenders for the LAMPS order are the Kaman SH-2D, a redesigned model of the UH-2 rescue and utility aircraft which has been in service for nearly ten years, and the Lynx, to be licence-built in the United States by Sikorsky Aircraft as the 'Sea Lynx' if selected as the LAMPS programme aircraft. The Lynx is slightly smaller and considerably lighter than the SH-2D—its normal take-off weight is less than the SH-2D's empty weight, a considerable advantage for operations from a small ship, where considerations of deck strength and top-weight are important. To bridge the gap between the present and the first deliveries of the successful LAMPS design, the United States Navy has ordered 20 SH-2Ds for use from its larger escorts.

The French Navy has a smaller requirement numerically, for a light helicopter. The destroyer *La Galissonnière* was completed in 1962, equipped with an ingenious flight deck and folding hangar arrangement. Three other destroyers have since been fitted or built with a flight deck, and these will operate Lynxes in place of the Alouettes currently in use.

One other NATO Navy, that of Italy, has pursued an independent path. In the late 1950's, two classes of escort vessel, the 'Bergamini' class frigates and the 'Impavido' class destroyers were ordered, and development of a light weapons-carrying helicopter commenced by the Agusta company, which had hitherto produced Bell helicopters under licence. The ships were completed between 1961 and 1964, but the definitive Agusta A.106 did not fly until early 1966, entering production in 1968. In the interim, the six ships operated Agusta-Bell 47 J3s—basically a commercial aircraft modified to carry a homing torpedo. The single-seat A.106 is the smallest and lightest of all the manned ASW helicopters, but apart from a limited freight capacity with an underslung load, it cannot be regarded as a utility aircraft.

The manned light ASW helicopter has proved to be as much of a tactical success as the medium aircraft. The Wasp has accumulated over 125,000 deck-landings in nine years of operations from 54 ships and according to a recent Westlands/Aerospatiale advertisement, there have been only six deck-landing 'incidents'. One hundred Lynx's are on order for the Royal Navy, and another 80 for the French Navy; the former will embark in Type 42 destroyers and Type 21 frigates initially, while the French require an aircraft to equip existing ships. If the LAMPS contract is awarded to Sikorsky, then a production run of over 600 aircraft—Lynx's and Sea Lnyx's—is not over-optimistic.

HMS Rapid

P. A. VICARY

HMS *Rapid* launched on July 16, 1942 from Cammell Laird's yard, formed part of the Emergency War Destroyer programme, and was completed on February 20, 1943. Armed with four 4.7in, two 4pdrs, eight 20mm guns, and eight 21in torpedo tubes, she went straight into war service with the Home Fleet, joining the escorts of a troop convoy bound for the Middle East.

In 1944 she underwent a short refit, after which she went to the Far East to join the Eastern Fleet in operations against the Japanese, and formed part of the escort to a convoy which was conveying the 14th Army bound for Burma. She then performed gunnery support missions during the bitter offensive at Arakan. While bombarding shore batteries the *Rapid* received a hit amidships causing many casualties and bringing the ship to a standstill. She was towed clear of the shore batteries, and after repairs by her crew, managed to raise steam on one boiler and bore away at 20 knots. After repairs the *Rapid* took part in the re-occupation of

Singapore, and at the conclusion of the war in the Far East she returned home to Britain. She re-commissioned at Rosyth in 1946 and joined the Rosyth Escort Force where she remained until 1947, when she steamed south to join the Local Portsmouth Flotilla. In 1951 the *Rapid* was paid off for conversion to a fast anti-submarine frigate, and upon completion, after running trials, was placed in Reserve. In 1956 she was placed on the sales list. The Ecuadorian Navy showed interest in the ship, and she ran a trial trip in the Solent, but the deal fell through.

Late in 1966, after being in Reserve for about 13 years the *Rapid* was steamed to Rosyth, where her armament etc., was removed, and she became a training ship for Engine Room Artificer Apprentices, as tender to HMS *Caledonia*.

During June 1971 the Commanding Officer of HMS *Rapid* (Lt. Cdr. W. Kelly, RN), with the full agreement of the Ministry of Defence, agreed with the commanding Officer of HMS *Cavalier* (Cdr. C. Snell, RN) to have a friendly race to see which ship was the faster. The *Rapid* was firm favourite with the slogan 'Rapid by name and Rapid by nature'. July 6, 1971, being a fine day with a smooth North Sea, the two ships left the Forth and sailed north to the starting point, off the Scottish coast. The two ships worked up to full speed as they steamed south for about two hours, covering a distance of 74 land miles. Both ships were travelling at about 33 knots, with the *Rapid* leading, when about half way,

HMS *Rapid* after steaming south to become a member of the Portsmouth Local Flotilla in October

1947. She is seen here with her original Pennant Number. *[P. A. Vicary*

owing to the accidental lifting of a safety valve in the *Rapid*, a serious loss of pressure occurred as steam escaped. The *Rapid* began to lose her lead of about 100 yards, and the *Cavalier* began to catch up. As they ran neck and neck towards the end of the race the *Cavalier* took the lead and became the winner by about sixteen yards. The *Rapid* is still attached to Rosyth continuing her useful work as a training ship.

Top: HMS Rapid in Reserve in September 1960. She has been converted from a destroyer into a fast anti-submarine frigate. *[P. A. Vicary*

Above: HMS Rapid as tender to *HMS Caledonia.* Note removal of forward 4-inch gun and height-finding radar aerial. Aft the director and 4-inch guns have also been removed. *[MoD, RN, Official*

129

The 1972 Defence Estimates and the Royal Navy— A Critical Survey

ANTHONY J. WATTS

The publication of the Defence Estimates in February 1972 has done little to ease the minds of those who were looking for a significant increase in the operational strength of the Royal Navy. Conservative Governments have traditionally been the champions of strong, well balanced, Armed Forces. The present Government, however, strongly conscious of the need to combat growing inflation, and of the need to strengthen the economy by reducing public expenditure wherever possible, has not pursued such a strong Defence policy as has some of its predecessors. Ever since the end of the Korean War the strength of the Royal Navy has slowly declined. The abolition of conscription, and the difficulty of attracting the required numbers of voluntary recruits of a sufficiently high standard of education needed to operate and maintain the ever increasing complexity of the equipment used by the Royal Navy, has caused severe manpower problems within the service. Numerous schemes have been devised to overcome this acute problem, which may, I fear, remain for some years to come, especially as more complex vessels requiring larger numbers of highly trained technicians join the Fleet. The other major problem confronting the Navy has been the continually increasing cost of materials and equipment. Various factors, such as higher wages, increasing costs of raw materials, the increasing complexity of equipment entailing more complex production techniques etc., etc., have caused costs to escalate astronomically over the last two decades.

To begin let us examine the overall defence policy set down in the 1972 Estimates. After coming to power in June 1970 the Conservative Government published a Supplementary Statement on Defence Policy. Under the previous Labour Government, the Armed Forces of Great Britain had been severely curtailed as part of a continuing Labour policy to reduce the overall strength of the Armed Forces in an endeavour to promote world disarmament (Defence does not form one of the major factors in Labour Party Policies) and in an attempt to cut public expenditure. The Conservative statement set out to define the future defence policy of the new Government. One of the first priorities was to make a critical examination of the state of the Armed Forces, and to review future defence objectives and priorities. Keenly conscious of the continuing need to curb inflation the Government also set out the future levels of Defence expenditure.

Previous Defence Estimates, by their continual reduction in expenditure and, in the view of some people, mistaken priorities, had left Britain's home and overseas security in a parlous state of affairs. One of the main responsibilities of Britain's Armed Forces is to share, with her allies, in preserving the peace and stability of the world. Owing to previous Defence cuts, Britains' share in this vital role had fallen by 1970 to a dangerously low level. The Conservative aim was to improve the capabilities of the Armed Forces in carrying out this role. Coupled with this aim was a strong determination to overcome the manpower problems from which all three services were suffering, and to improve their public image, bringing to the notice of the general public the importance of the maintenance of adequate strength in the Armed Forces.

These plans, would, of course, cost money, a great deal of money, and the Conservative problem was to fulfil the objectives they had laid down, and yet still keep the yearly Estimates within economically sound limits.

The main strength of Britain's forces lies in the North Atlantic Alliance. This was, and still, is, the first priority of our Defence policy, and to this end the British deterrent, vested in the four Polaris submarines of the Royal Navy, forms our main contribution to the Western strategic deterrent. Apart from the Polaris forces Britain also contributes a 'County' class destroyer and two frigates to the SACEUR force stationed in the Mediterranean, and these are backed up from time to time by a carrier and amphibious forces. In addition to this all the vessels of the Royal Navy are assigned to NATO in a case of a general emergency.

Britain, however, has other commitments apart from NATO. We have world wide trading and political interests, and we depend on stable conditions to maintain these interests. Any threat to this stability must be countered, as far as our resources will allow. With the reduction in our Armed Forces, and more particularly the Royal Navy, which has now been concentrated under one command in home waters, the Conservative Government set about forming a Five-Power Commonwealth Defence Agreement to maintain a force in the Far East. The 1972 Defence Estimates confirm that this has now been achieved and Great Britain, Australia, New Zealand, Malaysia and Singapore maintain an armed force in the Far East under a single command, called ANZUK, to which Great Britain contributes about six destroyers or frigates. This command has taken the place of the former British forces in the Far East which were withdrawn in November 1971. Opposed to the ANZUK force is the ever growing might of a well balanced Russian Navy, which now makes regular incursions from the Pacific into the Indian Ocean, an area almost devoid of Western forces. At the moment these incursions remain only temporary visits, for the Soviet Navy has no permanent bases in the Indian Ocean, but for how long this state of affairs will last is uncertain. Russia has already made a number of so far unsuccessful attempts to secure base facilities in this area. I said above that any threat to political or economic stability must be countered as far as our resources will allow.

The last phrase in this sentence is bound, however, to cast doubts in the minds of some, as to whether in fact our present resources are in fact sufficient to meet this threat in the Far East.

In addition to the foregoing contributions to NATO and ANZUK, British warships are regularly detached to exercise with CENTO and SEATO forces, with whose member countries we have defence agreements.

In the strategic field then the defence aims of the Conservative Government have been attained, albeit at a very low level. It is true that great cost savings have been accomplished by withdrawing from overseas bases, but it can be argued whether, in view of the present world situation (the continuing tension in the Middle East and expansion of the Russian Navy in this area, the tension in the Far East between India and Pakistan, the Vietnam War which still drags on, and, again the growing Russian Naval presence in these areas, and latterly problems in the West Indies and Persian Gulf) our withdrawals from overseas bases has been a wise move.

Turning to the actual *material* contribution of these agreements and the strength of the Royal Navy, matters are not quite so healthy. The main point of discussion which everyone has looked for in the 1972 Estimates has failed to materialise—namely a definite order for the new Through-Deck-Cruiser (TDC), which will replace Britain's carrier force. There is not space here to go into all the arguments for and against the policy of phasing out the carriers, but at the time there were many who hoped that when the Conservatives came to power the folly of removing these valuable warships from the Fleet would be reversed. Unfortunately this was not to be. The *Eagle* is now preparing for scrap, leaving only the *Ark Royal* to remain in service until the late 1970's. Manpower problems, claim the Conservatives, have forced them to proceed with the original plan to decommission the *Eagle*. This has now left a very serious gap in our defences, for if the *Ark Royal* ever has to be taken out of service for refits, or as a result of unforseen accidents etc., then there is nothing to take her place and provide air defence for the Fleet and ground support for any amphibious operations. The RAF, due to a severe shortage of aircraft, has stated, and also unfortunately proved during Exercise Highwood in December 1971, that it cannot provide both air cover for the Fleet (even if this were operationally feasible in a sudden emergency overseas far from a suitable base) and defence of the United Kingdom, the latter being the first priority of the RAF. For the moment then, a large part of the Fleet is devoid of any effective form of air cover or distant defence against enemy aircraft. Nor is there any likelihood of the situation being eased in the near future by the addition of a TDC capable of operating V/STOL aircraft. All that the 1972 Estimates state is that a further contract has been placed to finish the remaining *preparatory* work on the design. If this is only *preparatory* work on the design then it will be well into the 1980's before the first of these vessels becomes fully operational. Apart from this it has not yet been officially stated that the TDC will operate V/STOL aircraft although the Navy is keen that the vessel should have V/STOL capabilities. In spite of this, however, the vessel begins to look more like a fully fledged carrier every day. From an initial conception of developing the *Blake* helicopter cruiser idea it has progressed to a vessel with a flight deck the full length of the ship and capable of operating VTOL aircraft. The latest pictures and models of the proposed vessel show the addition of an angled deck to enable the TDC to operate a new generation of V/STOL aircraft—aircraft such as the Anglo-French Jaguar now under development, and derivatives of the Harrier. If the TDC is completed on the lines of the model then she will be able to some extent, relieve the RAF from the duties of providing the Fleet with air cover.

The main difficulty would appear to lie with the aircraft which will presumably operate from the TDC. Trials have shown the Harrier to be a suitable type of aircraft for this development, but the 1972 Defence Estimates have proved most disappointing in this respect. The Estimates state that no suitable V/STOL aircraft at present exists for maritime use, and further they give no indication that the Harrier will be developed into such an aircraft. They do poin to two courses open to the Defence Ministry—either to design a new aircraft, or to develop the Harrier. If designs have proceeded so far with the TDC surely the course is plain enough to see—the Harrier must be developed for maritime use. This will take time, but less time than it would to design, develop and test a completely new aircraft (the first VTOL flew in October 1960, the production order for the Harrier was placed in 1967 and the Harrier had its first full scale naval trials in 1971). If the Harrier is not developed now, then the RAF pilots, who would presumably operate the aircraft from the TDC, will not have gained the necessary experience in operating V/STOL aircraft from a moving deck, using the *Ark Royal*, to be able to operate more or less straight away from the new TDC when it is commissioned. (A further point against decommissioning the *Eagle* is that the highly trained deck crews will be lost, and new crews will have to be trained from scratch for the TDC). Thus we shall have a TDC but no fully operational V/STOL squadrons capable of operating from it, and so her full potential will probably not be developed until some time after she has joined the Fleet. A very serious state of affairs, assuming of course that the Royal Navy intends operating V/STOL aircraft from the new TDC. The 1972 Estimates admit that development of the Harrier would also be quicker and cheaper than developing a new aircraft and that studies of the problem are being pressed forward. 'Careful examination of all the issues involved is needed before a final decision can be made', state the Estimates. Thus it would appear that another year at least will elapse before we see any concrete statement regarding the practical development of a naval V/STOL aircraft. We need to quickly develop the Harrier as an interim aircraft while at the same time pressing speedily forward with studies on a completely new V/STOL aircraft. Perhaps it is that a final Conservative and Ministry of Defence policy regarding naval aircraft has still to be settled.

It is now generally acknowledged that the aircraft carrier no longer holds pride of place in a fleet; the nuclear-powered hunter-killer submarine is the capital ship of today. The Royal Navy now has seven of these submarines in service with three more under-construction, and one to be ordered during the coming year. (America has 75 such vessels and Russia 20). In addition there are 21 modern diesel/electric submarines of the 'Porpoise' and 'Oberon' classes (the remaining five submarines of the 'A' class have reached the end of their useful life and are now being decommissioned and scrapped). In submarines the Royal Navy is woefully weak, especially in the nuclear-powered hunter-killer category. There is, however, an improved class of nuclear-powered hunter-killer submarine under design for the Royal Navy, but in view of the time it will take to complete the vessels of the 'Swiftsure' class (probably between five and six years), the rate of ordering of such vessels (one or at most two such craft per year), and their ultimate cost (*Courageous* will cost about £29.3 million, over £10 million more than the *Dreadnought*), it will obviously be quite some time before we have anything like an adequate fleet of these vessels, and by that time our remaining diesel/electric boats will have reached the end of their useful life. It is difficult to see how the rate of construction of these highly expensive vessels can be increased and at the same time maintain the overall balance of the fleet while keeping the Estimates within the levels the Government has set. If the Government keeps to the level of expenditure already set down, then hunter-killer submarines can only be constructed at the expense of surface craft, and we are desperately in need of these latter craft as well.

It is in fact in the destroyer and frigate categories where most progress has been made in the 1972 Estimates. Here, however, deletions from the operational fleet are reducing the effective numbers quicker than new craft can reach the Fleet. At the moment six Type 42 destroyers are under construction, while it is planned to order one more during the year (only one?). Eight Type 21 frigates are under construction, but there is no provision in this year's Estimates for ordering further vessels of this class. Maybe this is because the Type 21 will be superceded by the Type 22 which is now projected and under design, but for which no orders are as yet contemplated. None of these designs has given space for the fitting of a suitable surface-to-surface missile. The October 1970 Supplementary Statement on Defence Policy stated that the French missile system EXOCET was to be introduced into the Royal Navy to cover a serious gap in our defences, first brought to light in 1967 (see J. Marriott's article on Surface-to-Surface). This serious gap still exists, and has been further widened by the withdrawal of the carriers, whose aircraft covered the surface attack problem. In spite of the 1970 Statement, EXOCET has still not been fitted to any British warships, and the best that the 1972 Estimates can offer is that the first missiles will be delivered sometime during this financial year. It is a great pity that the Type 42 and Type 21 vessels will not have the advantage of this weapon from the outset, but will have to be adapted to carry it later.

Turning to the deletions from the Fleet, I have already commented on the fate of the *Eagle*. Another notable vessel placed on the disposal list is the cruiser *Lion*. The three cruisers of the 'Tiger' class have led a very chequered career (see feature on the 'Tiger' class). Since their launching at the end of the Second World War these three vessels have spent the greater part of their lives, either in dockyard hands, or lying in reserve in some backwater. The conversion of the *Blake* to a helicopter cruiser has not been wholly successful, and on a cost basis (the conversion cost £5½ million) it can be questioned as to whether the conversion has served any useful purpose. The design of the vessels is obsolete (they were designed before the Second World War) and there is insufficient space in the vessels

The value of these vessels as helicopter cruisers can be further questioned on the grounds of what role they are to play in any future conflict. At present they operate as anti-submarine helicopter carriers and command vessels. They do not, however, fit into the A/S role, and this was not what they were intended for when they were converted. They are far too large and vulnerable a target to be used as A/S vessels, nor are they properly equipped for such a role. The original role of a cruiser is no longer applicable, cruiser duties these days being performed by general purpose frigates. Could they perform fleet defence duties? Again they are too vulnerable for this duty, and would themselves need protection from attack. Had they been converted to mount surface-to-surface missiles then there might have been some basis for their retention in the fleet. The only possible role these vessels can fulfil now is in amphibious operations, and here too they are not wholly suitable for the task. They can only carry four helicopters, far too few to be of any use in an amphibious operation, they cannot carry large number of troops, again a handicap, and although they can act as command vessels, the *Fearless* and *Intrepid*, with their Skynet satellite communications network, have been specially designed and fitted for this purpose and are far superior to the *Blake*. The *Blake* and her sisters could provide gunfire support for troops ashore and for softening up, but these tasks can equally well be covered by smaller destroyers and frigates mounting 4.5in guns. It would appear, therefore, that the 'Tiger' class vessels are of very little use, for although it has been decided to press on and complete the conversion of the *Tiger* to a helicopter cruiser this year, the *Lion*, which it had been planned to convert in the 1970 Estimates, has now been placed on the disposal list, for reasons it is stated, of economy in manpower. If the *Tiger* and *Blake* were also set aside, the saving in manpower and costs from all three white elephants would have been sufficient to have kept the *Eagle* in commission until the new TDC is completed.

Turning from problems of *material* to those of manpower, when the Conservatives took office in 1970 they found that the reduction in manpower planned by Labour had exceeded even the Labour Government's expectations, and the services were seriously understrength. This was due in the main to a serious drop in the recruiting figures. According to the 1972 Estimates the continuing decline in manpower has at last been arrested, and over the last year there has been a noticeable rise in the recruiting figures, in both the officer branches and the ordinary ranks. In addition the number of Servicemen re-engaging has increased. With the time taken to train men to operate the complex electronic gear and machinery on board a modern warship this is a most welcome trend, which it is hoped will continue. In spite of this rather more happy situation, there are still manpower difficulties in some branches of the Navy, noticeable in the Engineering Mechanic, Communications and Electrical fields, this latter now being the most difficult in which to train a man. The increase in recruiting figures, may also suffer a setback during the next year when the school leaving age is advanced. At present the Services recruit almost their greatest percentage from the 15 year old age group (20 per cent). The answer to this problem lies in whether the Services can increase their quota of recruits from among the 16–17 year olds (from where they at present recruit 14 per cent and 23 per cent respectively), and whether they can encourage a larger number of men to re-engage after their present term of service has ended. To encourage potential recruits conditions of service have been greatly improved over the last year, and further improvements are planned for the coming year. The Services were awarded a 7% pay rise in August 1971 (applying to all ranks except senior officers of the equivalent of Major-General rank and above who were awarded slightly less). The biennial review in April 1972 has since awarded the services an average pay rise of $11\frac{1}{2}$ per cent. The rates of various additional payments (such as extras awarded to flying crew, submariners, divers etc.) are also under review, as are charges for food and accommodation. A further incentive to re-engaging has been the increasing popularity of the shorter term of engagement. During the period of the 1970–71 Estimates the percentage of men in the Royal Navy re-engaging, having completed a term of nine years, was 36 per cent. Over the first six months of the 1971–72 Estimates this rose to 45 per cent, and there is reason to believe this will continue to increase during 1972–1973.

Following the Report of the Donaldson Committee the Government put into effect on April 1, 1971, a scheme which allowed boys who enlisted before the age of $17\frac{1}{2}$ the right to shorten the length of the engagement for which they had opted, at the age of 18. After eight months of the scheme the percentage of boys in the Navy who decided to shorten their engagement was $28\frac{1}{2}$ of those who enlisted before the age of $17\frac{1}{2}$. The remainder confirmed their original intentions. After closely studying the problem of re-engagement a new system has been devised which will allow a man on completion of training, and after $1\frac{1}{2}$ years of productive service, to give 18 months notice of leaving the Service. Called Notice Engagement, this new system will be introduced on May 1st, 1972, and will form the initial engagement. The Donaldson Committee also recommended that Discharge by Purchase (now known as Premature Voluntary Release) be made easier for Servicemen. This has now been accomplished in the Royal Navy and the minimum qualifying period for release is $4\frac{3}{4}$ years. (This applies to a nine year engagement).

In order to increase the number of officers available for sea-going appointments a number of changes have been made in the training system. As from May 1972 the General Naval Training course at Dartmouth will be reduced from a year to under two terms. The entrants to the Seaman, Supply and Secretariat Branches, having undergone the General Naval Training, will proceed straight to a reduced period of academic studies in their particular branch at Dartmouth (or University if they so wish), before commencing their Fleet Training. Engineer officers will train for a degree at Manadon in one year instead of two, and having graduated, will then complete their Fleet training. The Operations and Warfare Course for Seaman Officers (normally lasting about 32 weeks) will be reduced by about a third and should be sufficient for the officer to carry out the duties of a first sea job during which he must obtain his Bridge Watchkeeping and Ocean Navigation Certificates. A new course will be introduced during the year known as the Principal Warfare Officer Course, the major part of which will be devoted to general warfare training. This course will give the Seaman officer a much broader insight into the conduct of modern warfare, rather than a profound knowledge in a particular type of action which previous subspecialisation has given after about seven or eight years in the Service. Lasting nine months the first of these new courses commenced at HMS *Dryad* in May, 1972.

On the research side, development of the SEA DART surface-to-air medium range and SEAWOLF surface-to-air close range missiles continues. These weapons will ultimately replace the SEASLUG and SEACAT and are the second generation of surface-to-air weapons designed for the Royal Navy. In addition to the continuing development of these surface-to-air weapons a new stand-off air-to-surface weapon is under development for the new Lynx helicopter. This missile will provide some measure of attack against enemy surface vessels, but is no substitute for supersonic carrier borne strike aircraft or a first class surface-to-surface missile. The helicopter is far too vulnerable a type of aircraft to carry air-to-surface weapons and would be shot out of the sky by surface-to-air missiles or aircraft long before it could get within range of an enemy surface warship. Another disappointing note concerns the Hovercraft. Yet again there is only the statement that the evaluation of this promising type of vehicle continues for naval purposes. Why is it taking the Ministry of Defence so long to make up its mind about the naval applications and capabilities of this versatile craft?

135

Finally what about Defence Expenditure for 1972–73? The total Defence Budget for the coming financial year is set at £2,854 million compared to a total of £2,722 million for 1971–72 (these figures have been corrected to relate to the present day value of the £). This shows an increase of £132 million over 1971–72 and an increase of £61 million over and above the target set for the 1972 Defence Estimates by the Government. The majority of this increase (£57 million) is accounted for by recent changes made in the accounting system of the Defence Budget. The remaining £4 million in the Estimates is covered by the cost of additional Nimrod aircraft (£3 million) and extra Defence orders announced on November 23, 1971, which were placed to stimulate employment (£1 million).

Out of the £2,854 million allocated for the 1972–73 Defence Budget the naval forces account for a total of £330 million, with the Polaris force costing an extra £38 million, a substantial increase over the 1971 Estimates. Of the £330 million allocated to the Navy, by far the largest sum represents the cost of the destroyer and frigate forces (£135 million), which are now being substantially boosted by new types of craft (Type 42 Destroyers and Type 21 frigates). The submarine force is allocated £51 million, again an increase on the 1971 Estimates. New construction again accounts for much of this. The cost of running the amphibious force has only marginally increased, while the carrier force (now only the *Ark Royal*) accounts for a mere £7 million (not including aircraft). Naval aircraft will cost £39 million during the coming year, and includes all types of aircraft—shore-based fixed-wing, and helicopters as well as aircraft for the *Ark Royal*. Comparing the 1971 and 1972 Estimates, the overall cost of running the Navy has certainly increased but part of this increase is accounted for by the ever decreasing value of the purchasing power of the pound. The only outstanding changes in the overall cost in the two Defence Budgets concerns the destroyers and frigates, and as I have already mentioned this is in part due to the new construction programme.

To conclude, there is little that is new in this years Defence Estimates, and it can only be hoped that the almost static situation with regards to the Navy will show some improvement in next years Estimates, with progress being made in the fields where I have noted deficiences.